Toy Making

Simple playthings to make for children

Gun Lee Blue

This book is dedicated to Oliver and Arlo Blue

Toy Making: Simple Playthings to Make for Children

© 2017 Gun Lee Blue

All pattern instructions, diagrams, and photos by Gun Lee Blue
Book design by Lory Widmer based on original design by Gun Lee Blue

ISBN: 978-1-936849-38-3

This publication was made possible by a grant from the Waldorf Curriculum Fund.

Waldorf Early Childhood Association of North America
285 Hungry Hollow Rd.
Spring Valley, NY 10977
845-352-1690 / info@waldorfearlychildhood.org
www.waldorfearlychildhood.org

For a complete book catalog, contact WECAN or visit our online store:
store.waldorfearlychildhood.org

All rights reserved. No part of this book may be reproduced in any form without the written permission of the publisher, except for brief quotations embodied in critical reviews and articles.

Contents

5   Foreword
9   Introduction
12   Dolls
42   Knitted Animals
58   Roly Poly
60   Play Crowns
62   Heavy Hen
72   Wool Balls
76   Resources
77   Patterns

"The most effective kind of education is that a child should play amongst lovely things.

—Plato

Foreword

When I was a child, watching my mother open her sewing basket was magical. That sewing basket was a treasure chest, and it didn't matter whether she was darning a sock or sewing a button on a shirt, I was captivated by what her hands could do. She often quietly sat by me as I played and sewed a dress for my doll, or repaired a hole in my favorite stuffed bear, and I could feel her love and interest in my world when she did this. It certainly can be overwhelming to consider making a toy by hand, and in today's world, it is so easy to go online and find the "perfect toy" for our children. There are many beautiful handmade toys that are easily obtainable from a variety of resources, but when a parent or caregiver has the opportunity to create a gift from his or her own hands, the toy somehow feels different. The love of the maker is expressed with each stitch, or click of the knitting needles.

As Renate Hiller, a well-respected handwork teacher and craftsperson, stated in a beautiful video entitled "Handwork" (available through Vimeo), "the use of the hands is vital for a human being to have flexibility and dexterity—in a way the entire human being is in the hand, our entire destiny is written in the hand." It is a sad but true reality that we are rapidly losing the capacity to use our hands in a purposeful way. I know young adults now who do not know how to use a hammer or sew a button on a shirt. As I sit here striking the keys on my computer, I can think to myself that this is a purposeful use of my hands, but in reality, it is a one-dimensional expression of the creativity and potential that exists in my hands.

Ms. Hiller goes on to say that, "Children grasp with their hand first, then they grasp with their mind. If they have had very little to grasp that is of the natural world, then what their mind grasps can be very little." Little by little we are losing the understanding of the value and meaning of things, especially when what we hold in our hands is artificial. An object made from natural materials beckons us to connect with it. How extraordinary it is that the natural object can absorb our own physical warmth, and then as we hold that object, our warmth and that of the object is passed back to us in return. There is a communication that takes place, which informs and nourishes our senses.

Handwork allows us to transform nature and make something truly unique. When working with our hands, we can find our center. Centering is an act of giving and receiving, and anyone who has tried to throw on a potter's wheel can attest to the importance of finding one's center. Working out of that centered place allows our individuality to be profoundly expressed through our creation. Handwork is a meditative experience for many, and by working with our hands to create something useful and beautiful, we can, as Hiller says, "find our way, by listening with our whole being."

How profound it is to consider, when doing handwork, the connections we have as human beings to the animal and plant kingdoms, as well as to other human beings. When we are knitting with a skein of wool, we can ask: who cared for and sheared the sheep that gave us this wool? Who washed and carded, spun and dyed the wool that we are using to make this object? In answering these questions we can no doubt begin to know why it is important to surround the developing child with materials that are natural and made by someone's hands. Certainly one can experience the warmth and interest that the maker has imbued into the object, and when it is made from one of nature's gifts, the connection becomes even more profound.

A toy that is handmade, rather than mass-produced, has a life of its own. A plastic or artificial toy often cracks, discolors, or breaks over time, and if left out in the elements, it will be less likely to be of any interest to the child. A toy of natural materials can be lovingly repaired, and if left out in the elements, can be resurrected by a good washing and a little fresh wool stuffing. All adults can make toys, the simpler the better, and less "perfect" is even better! It is the love and attention that went into the making of the toy that really stands the test of time. By paying attention to the color, texture, smell, and shape of something, one enables the young child to create an inner picture, and imaginative play will flow forth.

This simple and straightforward book of toy making for children, originally developed as a final project for the Waldorf Early Childhood Teacher Education program at Sunbridge Institute, is a perfect example of the connections author Gun Lee Blue has made—not only to the materials she used to lovingly create these toys, but also to the truth of what it is about a first toy that speaks so profoundly to a child. In the course of the program, she acquired a deeper understanding of child development and grasped how important it is to nourish the child's foundational senses—of touch, life, movement, and balance. She made profound connections to her final project proposal and subsequently set out to create and develop what I like to think of as a detailed guidebook. Her approach to making these toys is authentic and accessible to an audience who, like herself, never made these toys before. She made each pattern and worked through, step by step, each toy presented here. When something didn't work, she re-worked it, and found that making the pattern clear and user friendly, while difficult to achieve, was essential. As her project progressed, her home was transformed into a toy workshop, and unlike the shoemaker who went to sleep every night only to awaken to beautifully crafted shoes made by the elves, she spent many a sleepless night, after putting her children to bed, drawing, constructing, sewing together, taking apart and sewing again. She probably pricked her fingers more times than she cares to remember.

Many of these toys can be made in the presence of the child, perhaps even sitting bedside as the child falls asleep. The meaningful engagement of an adult in purposeful, creative work encourages and inspires young children in their play. The child will want to imitate your work, and perhaps even ask for a scrap of cloth or a piece of wool to create something for a beloved dolly. Often, when given a threaded needle, the child will sew until the thread is too short to pull through, and the fabric is in a tight-wadded ball. You then may hear, with great joy, "Look what I made!" Of course it is never the outcome, but the process, that matters. One can imagine that it would be a very special experience for the child to know that you are so interested in the world the child lives and plays in, that you would make toys for the child to play with. I remember clearly that the outfits my mother made for my dolls were really the most special ones to dress them in, and I took very good care of them.

When Gun presented her final project, and revealed a basket full of toys that she had created, there was a gasp of silence in the room. The audience could hardly wait to hold and cuddle each one. Love, interest, and pure intention were sewn into each one, and it was evident that everyone could sense that unique quality. I am confident that when one picks up this precious guidebook and sets out to create a handmade toy for a special child, those unique qualities will also be stitched into each one.

— Leslie Burchell-Fox

Introduction

There are many toys that are made of natural materials. But beyond being natural or eco-friendly, toys should be nourishing to the senses of the infant and the young child. It is important to surround children with toys that are handcrafted and inviting, toys that not only contribute to their sense of well-being (or "sense of life," as Rudolf Steiner, the founder of Waldorf education, referred to it), but also develop their aesthetic awareness and appreciation. Toys made with these principles in mind have a calming effect on children. A child is also much more likely to feel reverence for a beautiful handcrafted toy and care for it accordingly.

Rudolf Steiner suggested that children's toys should be largely unformed in order to stimulate a child's imagination. "Find toys and playthings that will be nourishing to our children, that stimulate their imagination and develop the sources of creativity and intellectual capacities that will develop in later years."[1] Waldorf toys are just that — simple without a lot of detail, open-ended in purpose. Baskets of wooden blocks and sticks, play silks, stones, shells, all can be transformed into a myriad of objects, allowing children's imagination free reign. Overly fixed and detailed toys can cause a child's imagination to diminish, since the way they play is determined by the toy itself. Children may also be confused and lost, not knowing what to do with a toy when it is over-stimulating.

Children naturally imitate adults and their daily activities through play. When mothers and fathers or adult caretakers model nurturing, caring behavior, children will imitate this in their play. Thus they also learn about relationships and empathy. Children need toys that are flexible and are able to grow with them.

Through play, children also develop the ability to regulate their emotions, process fear and anger, and build resilience. They learn to respect others and to see that the needs of others are as important as their own. During play, children learn to take an idea or an object and expand on it in a new way. To help children create, invent, explore, and imagine through play, we can provide toys that foster the creativity that evolves into creative thinking.

Toys must be developmentally appropriate, created with the needs of the child in mind. They should rely on the imaginative capacities of the unfolding child without imposing set directions. They should encourage meaningful creative play and assist children in their emotional, intellectual, and physical development. Making toys yourself will not only help you to encourage the unfolding of a child's imagination, it is an activity that in itself will also nourish and support the developing child, and can be inspiring and nourishing to you as well.

Providing developmentally appropriate toys is an aid to the child's incarnation in a physical body. "Because spiritual forces in the child first pass through the head (nervous-sensory system), then the heart (rhythmic system), and then finally the hand (metabolic-member system), the external forms of toys must correspond to the internal development process. At the beginning we find the head-like ball and the doll, then the stuffed animals, before finally materials from animate and inanimate nature (such as pieces of wood, fir cones, pebble stones, and sand) function as toys." [2] When children are able to take up, through play, the activities of adults observed in the environment, such as baking, gardening, building, and handcrafts, this also is a form of creative, imaginative expression that helps them to incarnate through the power of imitation.

Another wonderful aspect of making toys is being able to reuse old clothing or blankets you have stored away. How beautiful it is to turn an old receiving blanket into a baby doll, or an old sweater into an animal toy. Reusing a well-loved article of clothing or blanket makes it even more special for the child and for yourself.

Making toys will give you an opportunity to slow things down in your busy life, and you will find joy and peace through the creative process. There is something so special about making a toy by hand. Not only are threads and materials woven together, but love and care are intertwined in the heart of the toy. This wonderful gift will be cherished and can be passed on through generations. "In true education therefore the essential thing is to be able to bring an artistic element into our work and to apply it in the making of toys, for then we begin to satisfy the needs of the child's own nature." [3]

1 Rudolf Steiner, from a lecture given in Ikley on August 10, 1923, "Walking, Speaking, Thinking."
   In *A Modern Art of Education*, Lecture VI (SteinerBooks).
2 Heiner Ullrich, *Rudolf Steiner* (Continuum International Publishing Group 2008).
3 Rudolf Steiner, ibid.

Dolls

Waldorf dolls are soft and warm to the touch because of the natural materials used. When a child holds a Waldorf doll, the materials will absorb the child's warmth and can be soothing and therapeutic.

These dolls intentionally have minimal or even no facial features. The purpose of this simplicity is to encourage the imagination of the child. Young children play by imitating real life, and when a baby doll has a fixed, exaggerated smile, it is difficult for a young child to imagine the doll's range of emotions.

Finding ways to care for a doll "baby," in imitation of adults, can help children develop empathy, language, and social skills. "A doll is an image of a human being and is therefore the toy most suited to develop and enliven the self-image in the growing child," as Freya Jaffke tells us in her book *Toymaking with Children*.

When making a doll, keep in mind who the doll is for. Is it for an infant, or toddler, or a young child? Infants around three months old begin to reach out and grasp things that are within reach. A simple blanket doll is appropriate for infants who are learning to explore and play with their hands and mouths. Blanket dolls have unformed bodies and have knots that are inviting for chewing and gumming.

For a toddler around the age of two or three, an ideal doll is soft and pillow-like and huggable. Cuddly dolls are easy to grasp and hold. Sometimes they can be made with a bunting style that have closed bottoms (without legs), and usually have very little or no hair at all.

An older child around kindergarten age, whose motor skills are more developed, will enjoy a formed doll. These dolls have limbs and hair that can be played with, and interchangeable clothing with buttons, zippers, and snaps which further develop their fine motor skills.

Once you make one doll, you will want to make more! Making dolls in various sizes is wonderful fun for yourself and for the children.

Useful Stitches, Notches, and Snips

• Running Stitch: The needle goes up and down, in and out through the fabric layers that you would like sewn together. This is also the stitch to use for gathering fabric by gently pulling the thread after completing the stitching.

• Back Stitch: A circular movement takes each stitch backward on the underside of the fabric before progressing forward with the next stitch. This makes the seam stronger.

•Invisible Stitch: Also known as "ladder stitch" and "blind stitch." This stitch allows you to sew from the outside and not be able to see the thread once the stitching is complete.

• Notching and snipping on a curve: When creating curves on fabric, you will need to carefully notch on convex curves, and snip on concave curves. Be careful not to cut through the stitched threads. This will help keep the seams from puckering when the fabric is turned rightside out.

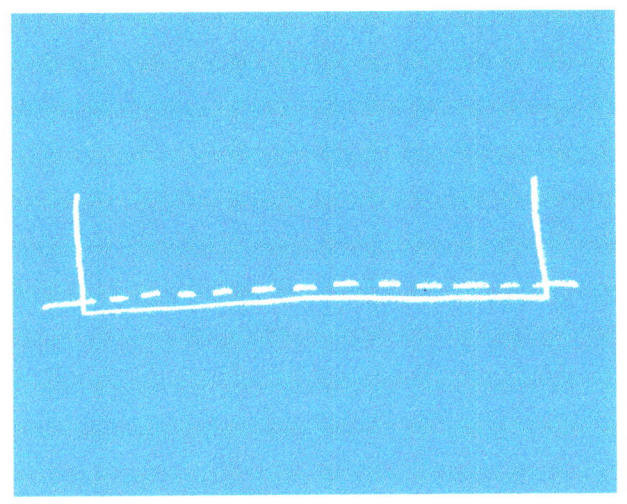
Running Stitch

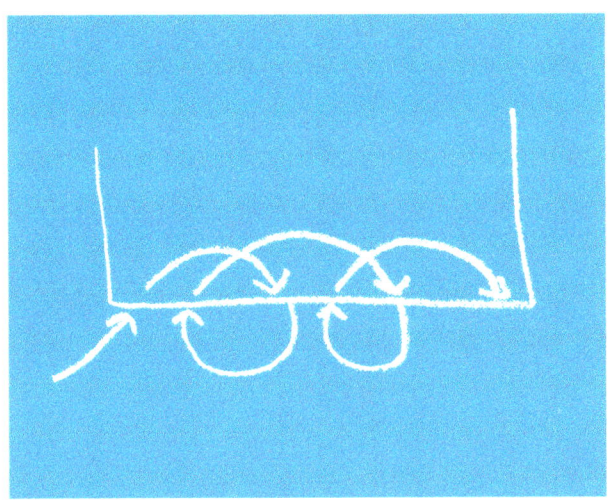
Back Stitch

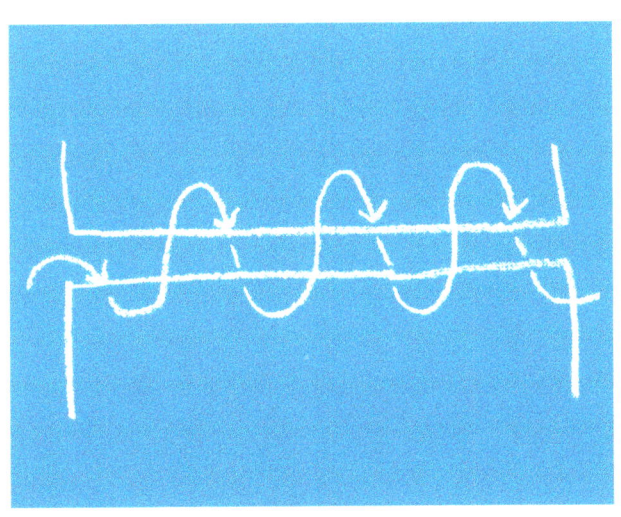
Invisible Stitch

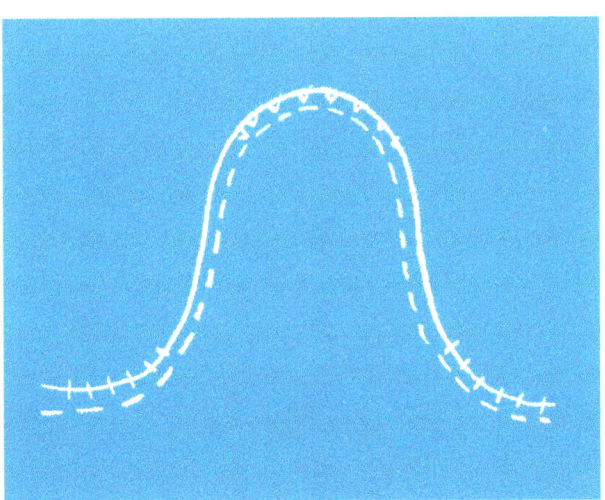
Notch and Snip

Dolls

Blanket Doll

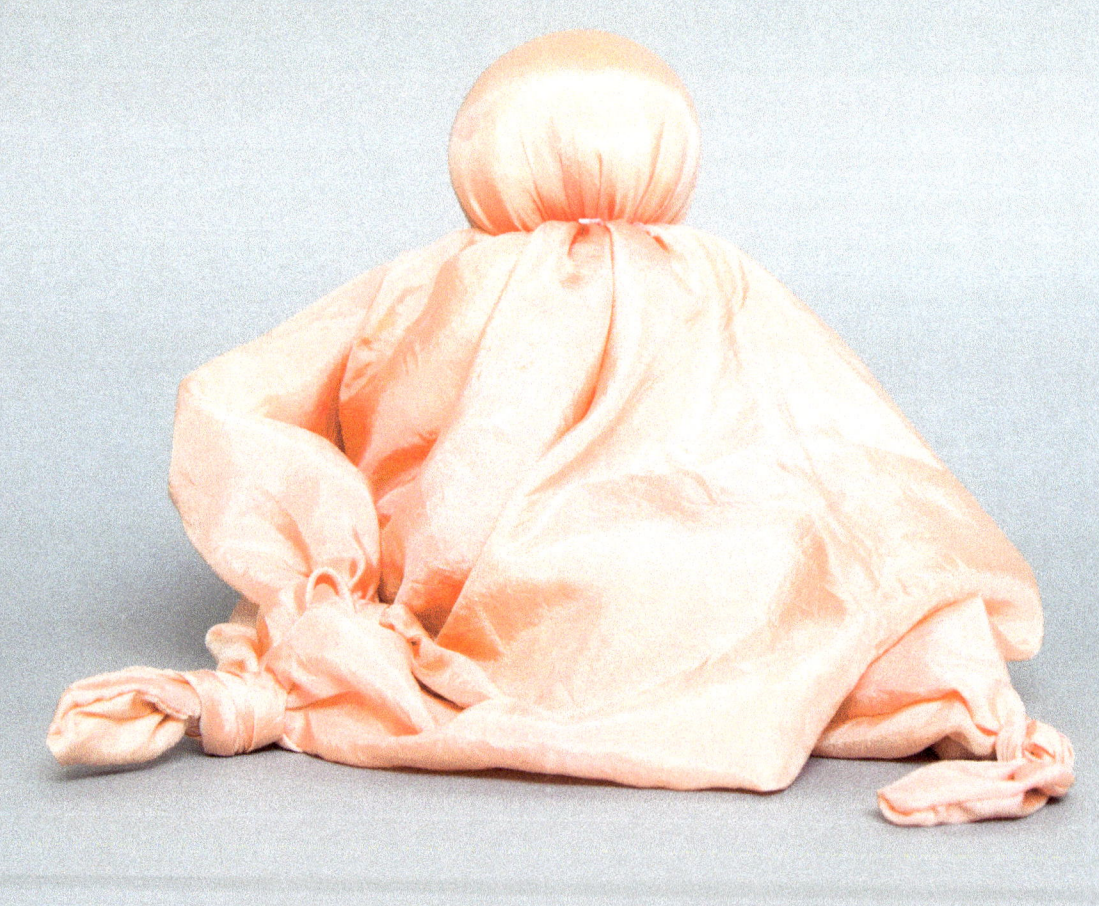

Toy Making 16

Materials

- Soft fabric: silk, cotton, or flannel
- Wool stuffing
- Strong cotton string
- Needle and thread

Step 1

Take a square piece of fabric and lay a tightly rolled up ball of wool in the center of the fabric. Gather around the ball to create the head and tie a cotton string around the ball to secure it.

Step 2

Sew together the edges and knot the ends.

Blanket Doll

Cuddly Doll

Materials

- Soft fabric: cotton, cotton velour, or flannel
- Cotton knit fabric (skin color)
- 2" stockinette tube (20" long)
- Wool roving
- Strong cotton string
- Needle and embroidery thread (same color as the fabric for body)

Step 1

Head—Sew one end of the stockinette tube, turn it right side out and set aside (fig. 1). Lay down two strips of wool roving in the form of a cross. Take a ball of wool and place it in the center where the strips of wool cross. Gather the strips of wool and wrap them around the wool ball. You may need to add more wool to reach the desired firmness and size. The head should quite firm, but yielding to the touch, and approximately 12.5 inches in circumference for a doll 15 inches in height. Place the tied end of the stockinette tube on top of the wool ball and roll the tube down to cover the head. Then tie a strong cotton string tightly around the neck (fig. 2). Make sure to tie a string at the bottom as well to keep the wool contained in the "muff" (the portion below the head).

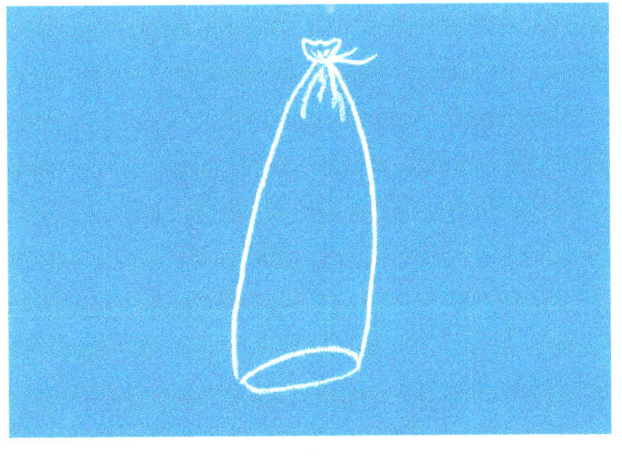

fig. 1

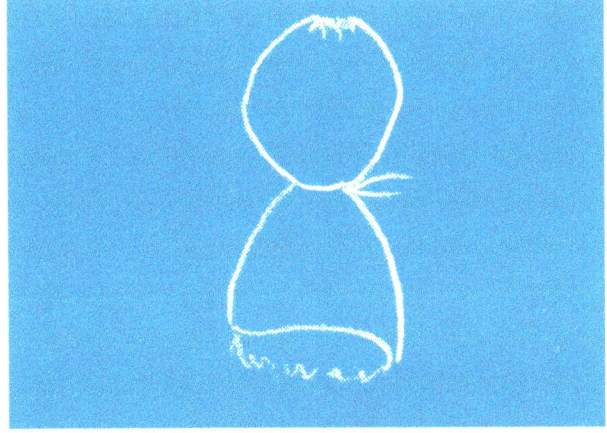

fig. 2

Cuddly Doll

You can leave the head like this and cover it with skin-colored fabric, or add indentations for the head. If you would like to create the indentations for the head, continue with the following directions:

Creating the head indentations

Keep in mind that pulling the strings to form the indentations for the head can cause cuts in your fingers, since you will be pulling hard. Be conscious while pulling, or protect your fingers with thin gloves or wrap with medical gauze.

Find the middle of the head, and tie a strong string around it, knotting it in the back. Locate the side where you wish the face to be. Reshape the wool, making sure the cheek and mouth areas protrude a bit farther forward than the forehead and look symmetrical. You can move the eyeline string to ensure proper facial proportions. Make sure the knot of the eyeline string is at the back of the head (fig. 3).

Taking another long strand of string, tie it on the side where one ear would be and pull it over the head towards the opposite ear. While keeping it pulled tightly, tie it around the eye line string to create the other ear area (fig 4). Then continue to pull the string tightly under the chin all the way across to the first ear area created, and tie again to anchor

fig. 3

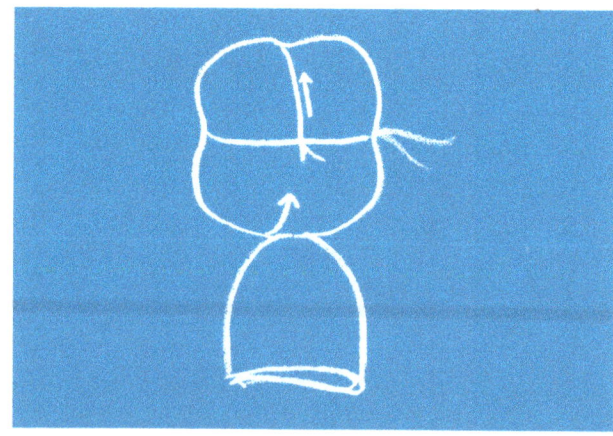

fig. 4

Toy Making

20

the string (fig 5). Pull down the eyeline string at the back of the head to create the nape of the neck and stitch it low on the back of head to secure. You have now created the indentations of a head (fig. 6).

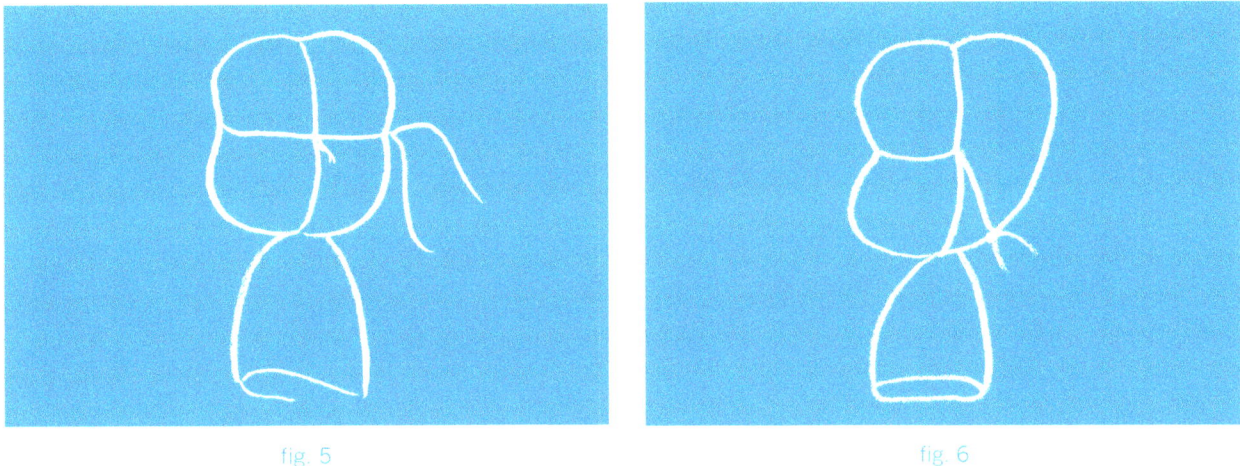

fig. 5   fig. 6

Step 2

Cut skin fabric according to the pattern. Sew one side leaving a little opening at the top and the bottom completely open (fig. 7). Turn right side out and place the skin fabric over the stockinette-covered head. It should be tight; you may need to adjust the skin fabric if you find that it is loose. Close the top of the head by using a running stitch and then pulling it to gather the fabric. Tie a skin-color embroidery thread around the neck (fig. 8).

fig. 7   fig. 8

Cuddly Doll

Step 3

Cut out the body and stocking cap from the pattern provided. You may need to adjust it so that it is proportionate to the head. Sew the body leaving an opening for the head. Turn right side out and stuff with wool so that it is soft like a pillow. Sew the stocking cap, turn rightside out, and set aside (fig. 9 & 10).

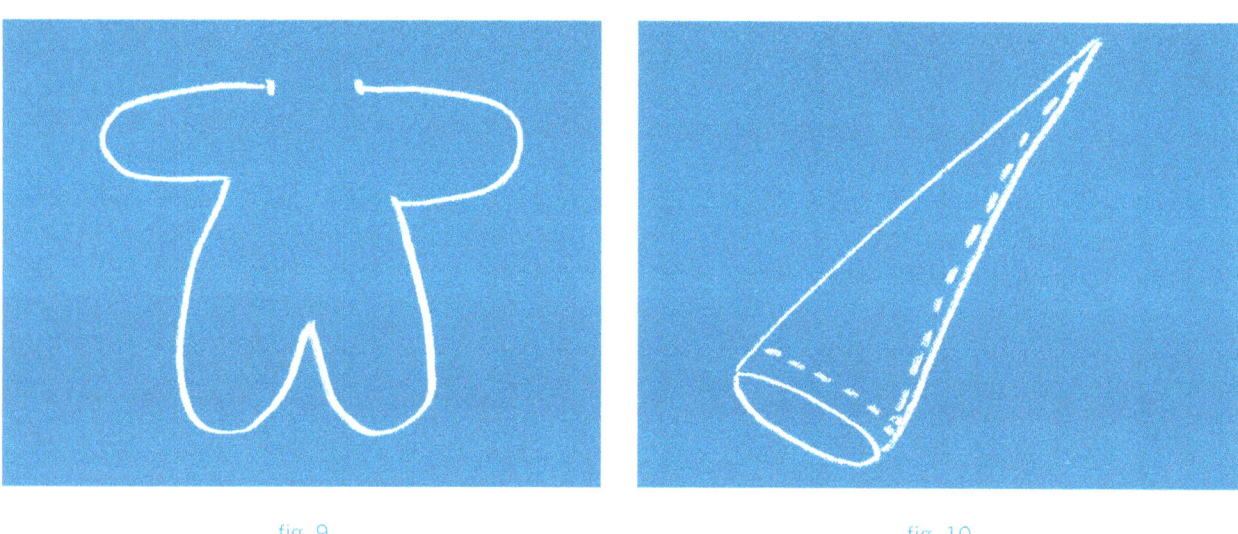

fig. 9   fig. 10

Step 4

Put the "muff" of the head inside the neck opening of the body and position it so that it is facing forward correctly. Sew around the body and neck using the invisible stitch, making sure the head is securely set into the body. With colored embroidery thread you can add little details for eyes and mouth or leave the face blank.

Toy Making

Step 5

Place stocking cap on the head and stitch directly onto the head. Tie the tip of the cap into a knot.

Step 6

Use a running stitch with embroidery thread to gather the fabric around the wrists and ankles by gently pulling to gather the fabric. This will create the hands and feet (fig. 11).

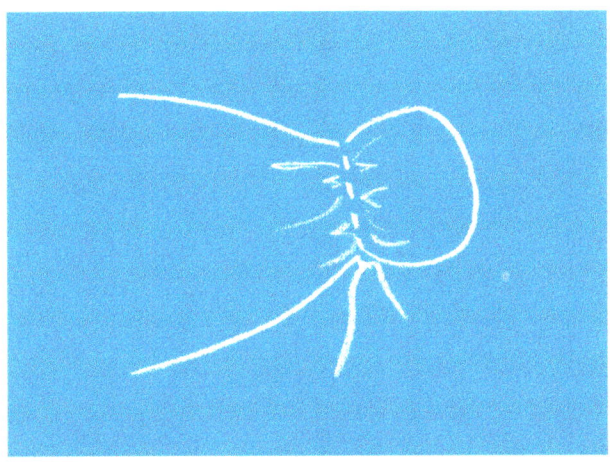

fig. 11

Cuddly Doll

Formed Doll

Toy Making 24

Materials

- Cotton knit fabric (skin color)
- 2" stockinette tube (20" long)
- Wool roving
- Strong cotton string
- Embroidery thread for eyes and mouth
- Yarn for hair
- Doll needle (very long needle)
- Needle and thread for sewing

Step 1

Head—Make the head using the same method as the "Cuddly Baby." Make sure you continue with the head indentation instructions from page 20. The head should also be approximately 12.5 inches in circumference for a doll 18 inches in height.

Step 2

Body—Cut the body and limbs according to the pattern. Sew the seams, leaving an opening for stuffing wool (fig. 1). Position the fabric of the feet as shown in fig. 2 and sew a curved seam to create the toe area.

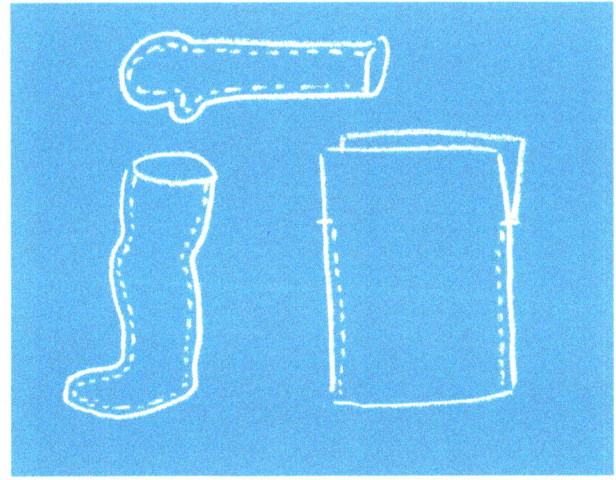

fig. 1

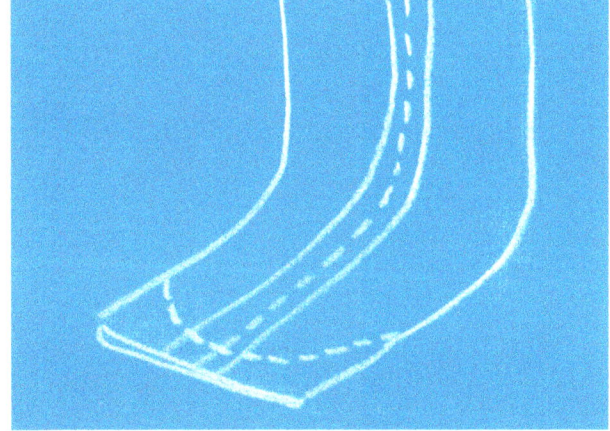

fig. 2

Formed Doll

Turn the arms and legs right side out and stuff with wool. Leave an unstuffed area at the end of each piece for attaching them to the body.

fig. 3

Step 3

Once the arms and legs are stuffed as firmly as you would like, keep the torso inside out and place the stuffed legs as shown in fig. 3. Pin and sew across where the top of the legs join with the torso. Turn the torso fabric right side out. You should see that the legs are placed properly.

Step 4

Place the head and the arms in position along the torso and adjust the length of the arms to proper length in proportion to head and body size. Attach the arms to the back of the "muff" (fig. 4). Place the joined arms and head into the open top of the torso. Make sure it is centered. Pin the torso fabric to the "muff" and sew all openings together, making sure to keep the head centered, facing forward, and secure (fig. 5).

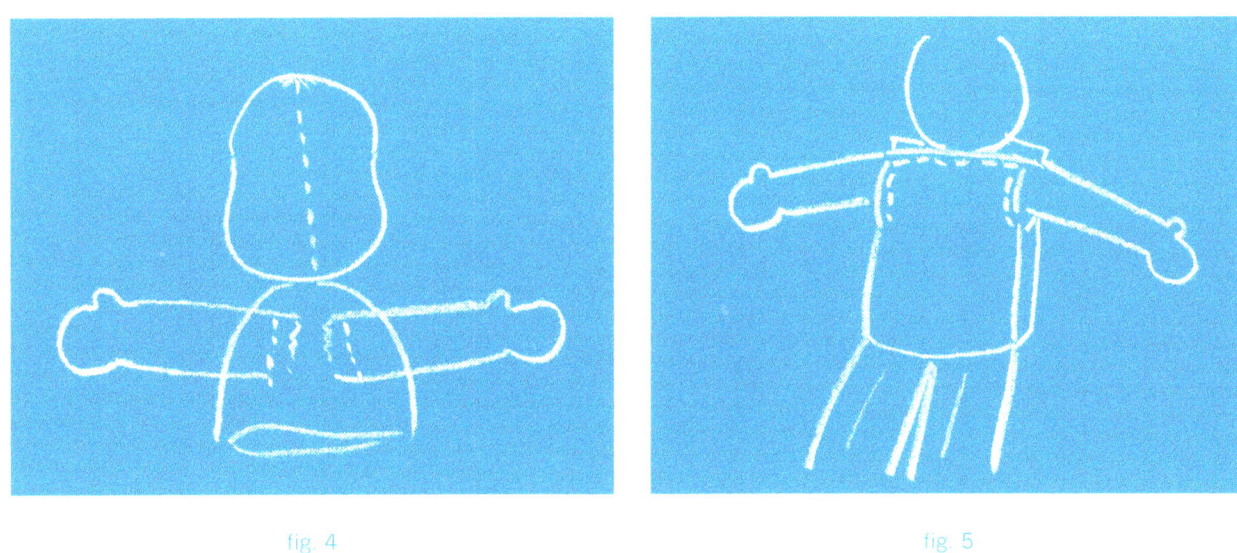

fig. 4   fig. 5

Step 5

Face—Use pins to mark the areas for the eyes and mouth, making sure the eyes and mouth are positioned properly and the eyes are along the eyeline indentation. Use colored embroidery thread to create simple eyes and mouth using a long doll needle, going in from the back of the head (which will later be covered with hair) and securing the ends there as well.

Formed Doll

Step 6

Hair—There are many methods for making doll hair. A simple way is to create a crocheted cap using mohair and combing the fibers out. Another is using a yarn crocheted cap and attaching it to the head, then tying strips of yarn randomly around the cap. The following images are examples of ways to make hair for the doll. Most of them involve using yarn and stitching it or attaching it to the head.

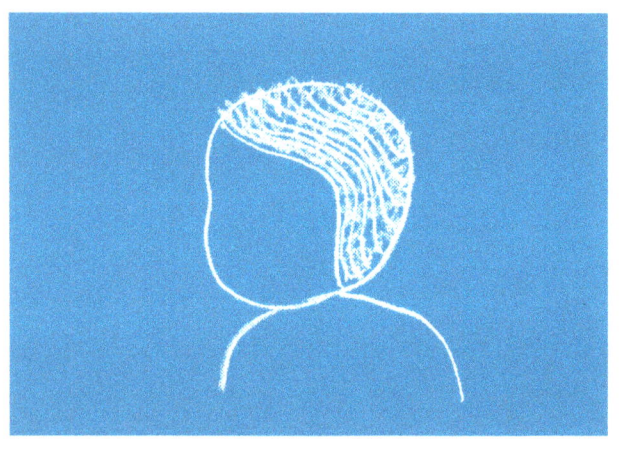

Crocheted cap

Crocheted cap with yarn tied

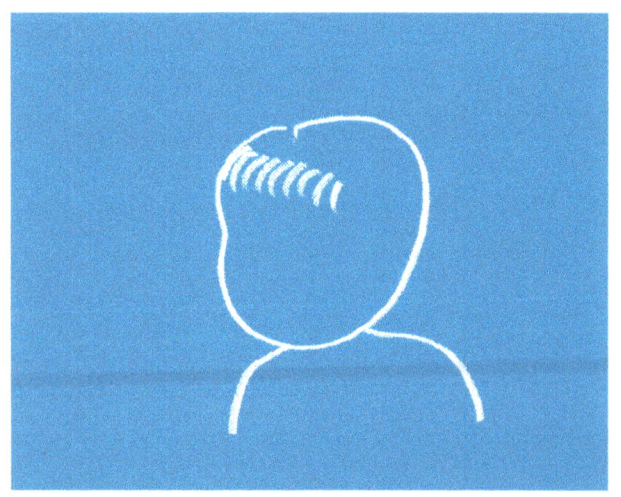

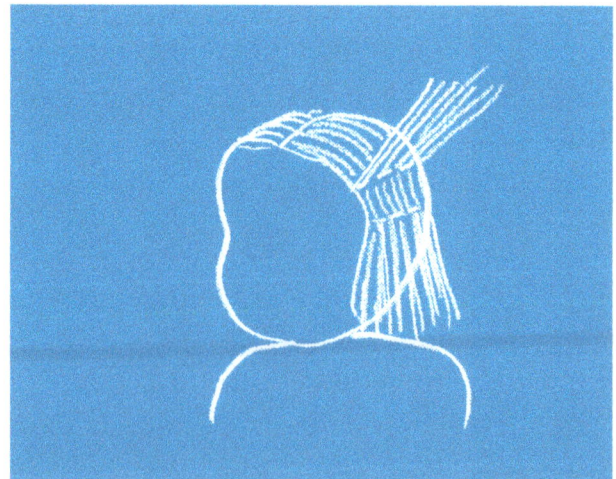

Bangs

Long hair (attached in layers)

Toy Making

Pony Tail

Straight short hair with part

Pig tails

Straight short hair

Formed Doll

Heavy Baby

The heavy baby doll is loved by children and adults because it feels like a real baby! The bunting style of the baby and the moldable weight of the body are soothing and comforting for the children while they are carrying and caring for the doll. A small two-and-a-half pound baby is appropriate for a nursery child. A large four-and-a-half pound baby is suitable for a kindergarten-age child. This baby has a removable and washable cotton velour fabric that is perfect for young children. You can fill the body with rice, millet, or even sand. Keep in mind that many children will tend to carry this baby by the head, so therefore the head needs to be extremely firm and securely attached to the body to prevent the neck from stretching.

Materials
- Cotton knit fabric (skin color)
- 2" stockinette tube (20" long)
- Wool roving
- Strong cotton string
- Embroidery thread for eyes and mouth
- Doll needle (very long needle)
- Muslin fabric
- Cotton velour fabric
- Rice, millet, or sand
- Funnel
- Button or snaps
- Elastic
- Ribbon
- Needle and thread for sewing

Step 1

Head—Make the head the same as the formed doll, using the head indentation instructions. The head should be approximately 12.5 inches in circumference for a small baby (14 inches in height), and 13.5 inches for a large baby. (16 inches in height). Use pins to mark the placement of eyes and mouth. The eyes should be placed along the eye indentation line. Stitch simple sleeping eyes and mouth.

Step 2

Body—Cut muslin according to the pattern provided in the Pattern section at the back of this book. Sew two pieces together with an opening at the neck. Do this again with the other two pieces of muslin fabric. You should now have two sewn-up bodies with openings for the neck. Take one of the body sacks and sew up the ends of the wrist openings (fig. 1). Do this with only one of the bodies. Turn the sack on which you did not sew the wrists rightside out. Place the sewn-up layer inside the other to create a two-layered body sack making sure the inner sack's wrists are sewn shut (fig. 2). Fold in the outer fabric along the wrist approximately 1/4 inch and iron.

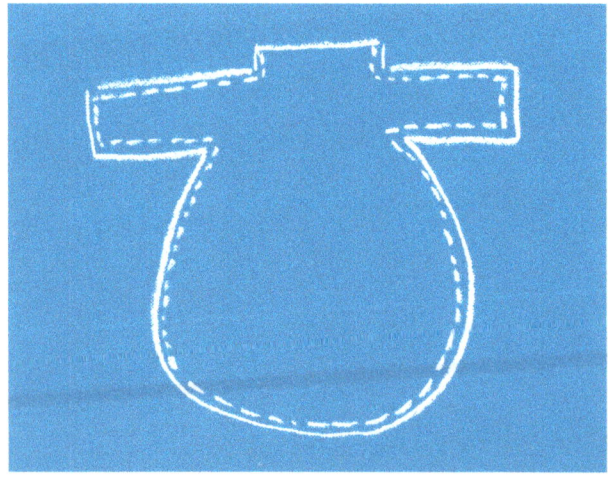

fig. 1　　　　　　　　　　　　fig. 2

Step 3
Using the funnel, fill the sack body using with rice, millet or sand to the proper weight.

Step 4
Holding the body carefully, preventing it from tipping over, place the "muff" of the head into the neck of the muslin sack and stitch together securely. There should be plenty of space between the weighted material and the neck.

Step 5
Hands—Cut the skin fabric according to pattern and sew. Turn the hands rightside out and firmly stuff the hands with wool and close off the ends (fig. 3).

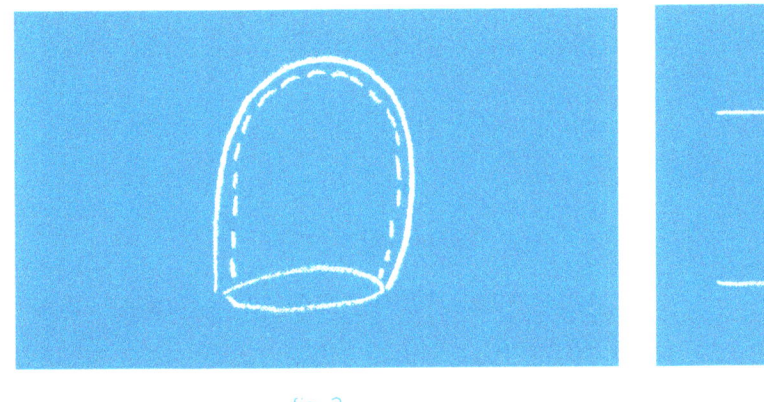

fig. 3

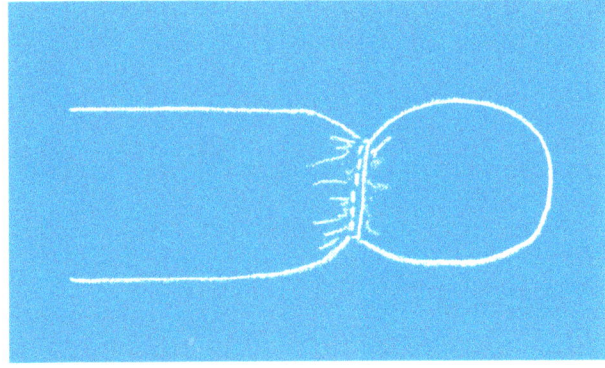

fig. 4

Step 6
Insert the hands into the wrists and sew the muslin onto the hands. Remember, you are sewing just the outer muslin fabric, not the part that has been sewn shut (fig. 4).

Step 7

Evenly place a small amount of the weighted material into each arm. Sew up the arms so that the weighted material stays in the arms. Do not make the arms full, just enough to make it flop (fig. 5).

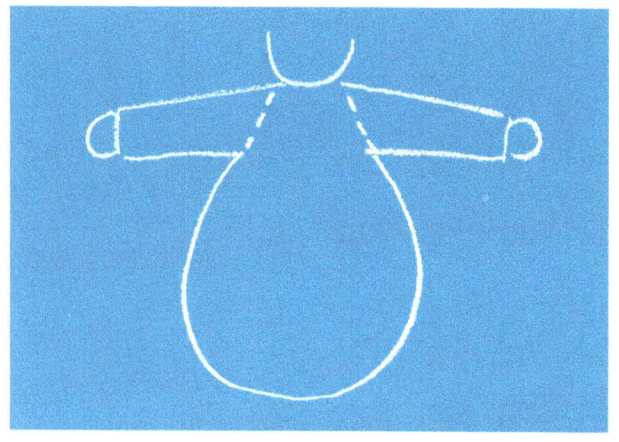

fig. 5   fig. 6

Step 8

Bunting and Cap—Cut the cotton velour fabric according to the pattern for the bunting and cap. Sew the sleeves onto the body of the bunting. (fig. 6). Then sew the sleeves and body, leaving the neck, wrist, and bottom open. Also leave about 4 inches of side seam open (fig. 7). This is for easy removal of the bunting for cleaning.

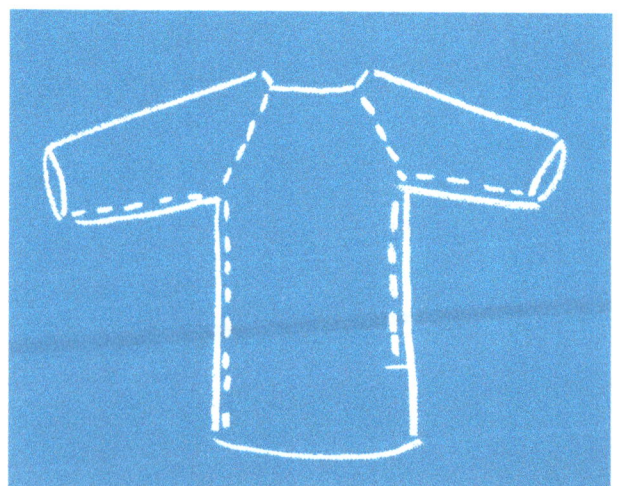

fig. 7

Step 9

Sew in elastic around neck, wrist and bottom of bunting. Attach a button or snap at the bottom corner (where there is an opening) (fig. 8).

Step 10

Cap—Sew the edges leaving the bottom open and hem stitch the bottom. Place on the head of the baby and adjust if needed. Then stitch onto the doll's head. Tie the open top closed with a ribbon (fig. 9).

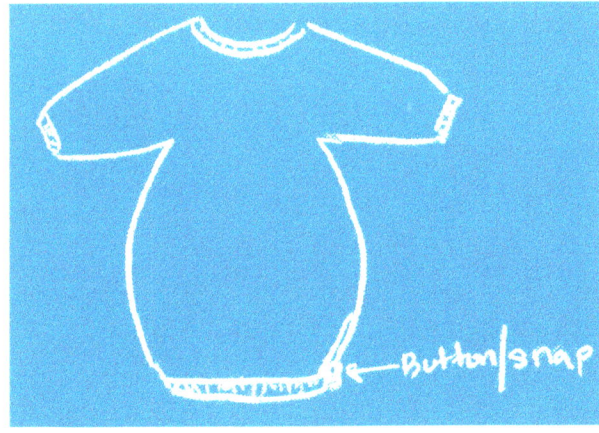

fig. 8

fig. 9

Knitted Dolls

Toy Making

These are simple dolls that can be made in a variety of sizes. The body is knitted in basic flat shapes. It is by sewing the seams together that you will form the body of each doll. You may want to explore using different thicknesses of yarn or a different number of stitches to make different body shapes and sizes. Knitted bodies are also forgiving because you can make adjustments while tucking and sewing the final body shape, which gives you a bit of room for alterations.

Materials
- Wool or cotton yarn
- Wool stuffing
- Cotton knit fabric (skin color)
- Needle and thread for sewing
- A tapestry or darning needle for sewing in yarn ends

Little Doll

Using a thin yarn and appropriately sized needles:

- Cast on 30 stitches, then knit for 8 rows.
- On the 9th row, knit 14 stitches and then bind off 2 stitches. Continue to knit the remaining 14 stitches of this row. This will create the hole for the head.
- On the 10th row, knit 14 stitches, cast on 2 stitches and continue to knit the remaining 14 stitches. You have now completed the hole for the head.
- Continue knitting for 7 more rows (rows 11–17).
- On the 18th row, begin by casting off 9 stitches, then continue to knit the remaining 21 stitches.
- On the 19th row, begin by casting off 9 stitches, then continue to knit the remaining 12 stitches, then increase 9 stitches.
- On the 20th row, knit 21 stitches, then increase 9 stitches. You should now see that you are back to 30 stitches.
- On the 21st row, knit the complete row.
- On the 22nd row, knit 15 stitches and place a safety pin or stitch holder on the remaining 15 stitches. You are now creating one of the legs.
- Knit the first set of 15 stitches for 18 rows. Cast off.
- Place one of your knitting needles back in the loops of the reserved 15 stitches and knit for 18 rows. Cast off (fig. 1).
- Fold the top down to create the arms and upper body along the head opening. Then fold the side of each leg toward the center to create the legs (fig. 2). Sew the edges together and stuff with wool. Add a small head stuffed with wool. Add a cap or bonnet and maybe even a tuft of hair!

Toy Making

fig. 1

fig. 2

Bunting Baby

Using a thick yarn and appropriately sized needles:

• Cast on 30 stitches, then knit for 44 rows

• On the 45th row, add 9 stitches by casting on, and then continue to knit the remaining 30 stitches. Then add 9 stitches by casting on. You should now have 48 stitches across. This will become the arms. Knit for 16 rows.

• On the 17th row of the arms, knit 21, then bind off 6 stitches, and then continue to knit the remaining 21 stitches. You will be creating the hole for the head.

• On the 18th row of the arms, knit 21 stitches, then cast on 6 stitches, and continue to knit the remaining 21 stitches. You have now created the hole for the head. You should also have 48 stitches across. Now continue to knit for 16 rows to complete the stitches and rows for the arms.

• Cast off 9 stitches, then knit 30 stitches. End this row by casting off 9 stitches. The stitches for the arms are now complete.

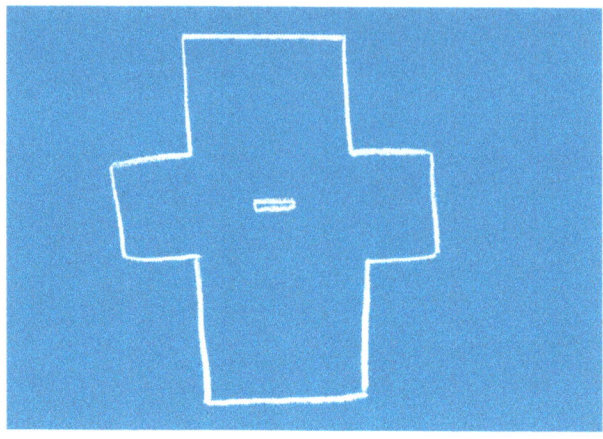

fig. 1

- Continue to knit the 30 stitches for 44 rows. Then cast off (fig. 1).
- Fold this knitted piece in half to create the arms and bunting body of the doll. Sew the seams with the same yarn leaving an opening for the hands and head. Then gather the bottom to create the bunting by using a running stitch and pulling gently to gather the bottom (fig. 2). Stuff with wool.

fig. 2

Toy Making

- Make a head similar to the Cuddly doll on page 19 and sew into the knitted body.
- Cut 4 pieces of skin fabric and sew together to create two hands. Stuff with wool and sew into the arms.
- To create the cap, cast on 50 stitches and knit for 35 rows. Then cast off. Fold the finished piece in half to create a square (fig. 3). Sew the back and place on the head of the doll and sew onto the head. Gather the bottom and stitch onto the doll (fig. 4).

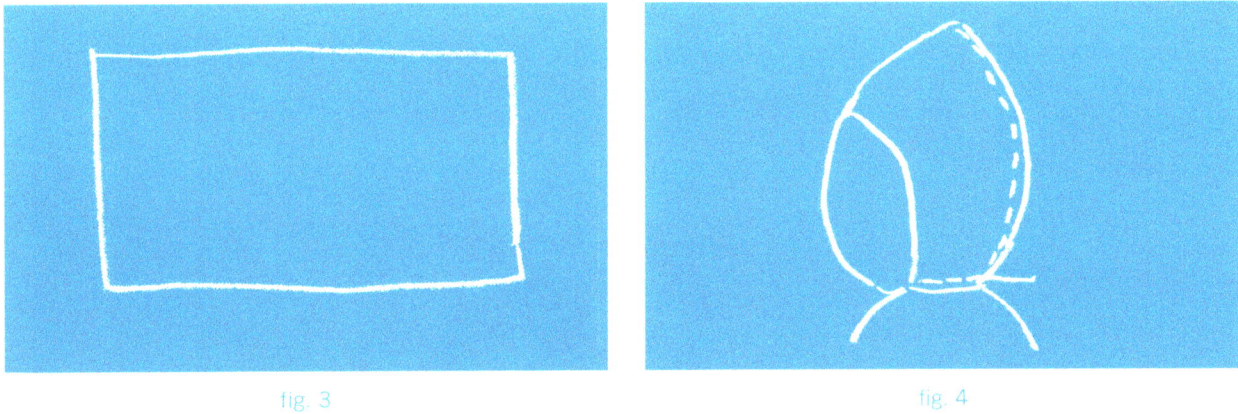

fig. 3 fig. 4

- Optional: Sew a running stitch with the same yarn all around the chest of the doll and gently pull creating a cinched chest area (fig. 5).

fig. 5

Knitted Dolls

Knitted Animals

These simple knitted toys are easy and fun to make. Children will love to hug these cuddly creatures and might even create their own puppet plays with them.

Knitted Animals 43

Rooster, Hen, and Chick

Materials
- Yarn
- Knitting needles
- Wool stuffing
- Tapestry or darning needle

Step 1

Cast on 20 stitches and knit every row for 20 ridges (40 rows) to form a square.. Cast off.

Step 2

Fold corner to corner to create a triangle. (fig.1) Sew the edges together leaving a little opening to stuff with wool. Then sew the remaining edge to close the opening. Take the same color yarn and sew from the bottom (point of triangle) up to the top of the back and sew back down to create the curve of the chicken (fig. 2).

fig. 1

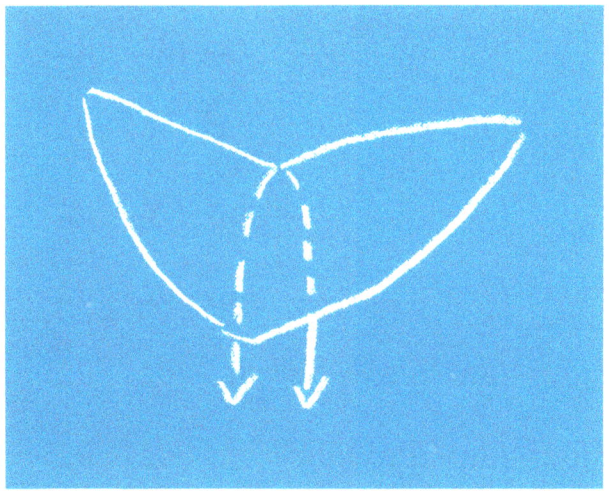

fig. 2

Step 3

Take a different color of yarn or embroidery thread to sew the eyes and beak. Use red or orange for the comb and wattle if making a hen or rooster. Tuck in loose yarn ends with a tapestry or darning needle. Create a feathery tail with short pieces of yarn if desired.

Rabbit

Toy Making 46

Materials

- Wool yarn
- Knitting needles
- Wool stuffing
- Tapestry or darning needle

Step 1

Body and Ears—Cast on 40 stitches. Knit every row for 40 ridges to form a square. Then cast off. For the ears, cast on 6 stitches and knit six rows, then decrease 1 stitch at the beginning of each row for four rows. Cast off (fig. 1).

fig. 1

Rabbit

Step 2

Shape the rabbit legs by sewing each corner of the knitted square together to create "cones" (fig. 2). Use a running stitch to sew across the cast-on/cast-off edge and pull lightly. This will create an area for the rabbit's head between the two front legs (top of fig. 3). Fill the head with a ball of wool. Tie yarn around the neck and knot to secure.

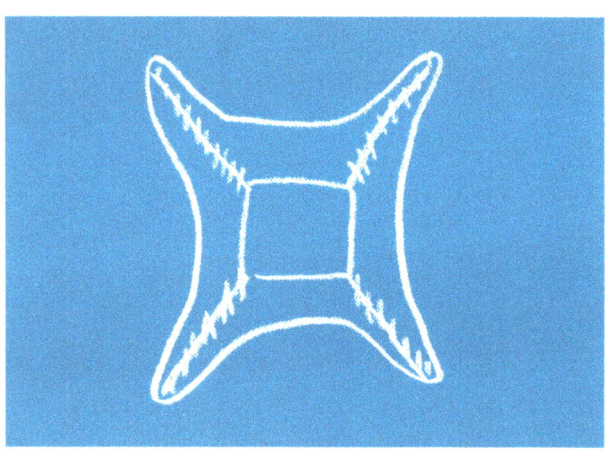

fig. 2

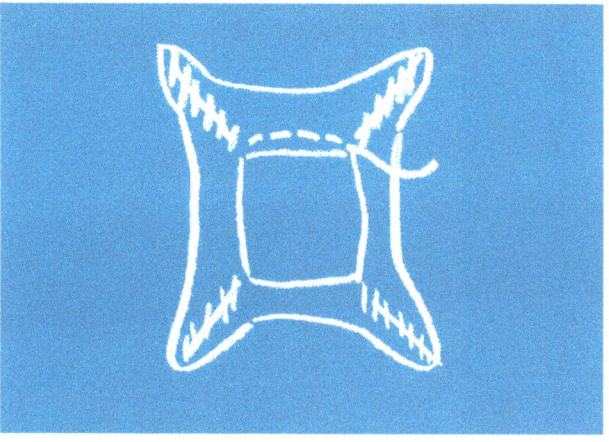

fig. 3

Step 3

From the neck, continue sewing a central seam down the stomach to the hind legs. Leave an opening for stuffing.

Step 4

Stuff the body and legs with wool. Then sew up the hole.

Toy Making

Step 5
Tuck hind legs close to the body and stitch in place. You can stitch the front legs together or leave them separate.

Step 6
Sew ears on top of head. They can stand up, or flop down.

Step 7
Make a tail— you can either sew short ends of yarn directly onto the back of the rabbit or create a pom-pom to sew on. To make the pom-pom, wind yarn around two fingers about 50-60 times. Pull off gently and tie a length of yarn around the center tightly (fig. 4). Cut the loops and shape and trim to desired look and size. Attach the tail to the back of the rabbit. Tuck in loose yarn ends with a tapestry or darning needle.

Optional: To create an indentation in the eye area, sew a couple stitches of yarn from one side of the head to the other.

fig. 4

Kitten

Materials
- Yarn
- Knitting needles
- Two double pointed knitting needles in same size if making I-cord tail
- Wool stuffing
- Tapestry or darning needle

Step 1

Body—Cast on 24 stitches and knit every row for 24 ridges to form a square. Or for a smooth (stockinette) surface, purl every other row, continuing until piece is square. Cast off.

Step 2

Head—Cast on 12 stitches. Continue knitting in garter or stockinette stitch and cast off when piece is the length of the body (fig. 1).

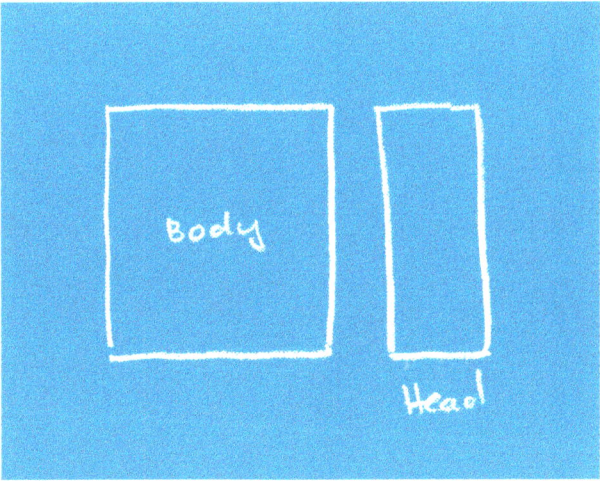

fig. 1

Step 3

Body—Fold the corners toward each other to create a "cone" for each leg. Leave an opening at the belly for stuffing (fig. 2).

Step 4

Stuff the body with wool firmly pressing into the legs. Then sew up the opening at the belly of the kitten.

Step 5

Head—Fold the head in the middle to create a square. Sew up the sides leaving the bottom open. Stuff with wool (fig. 3).

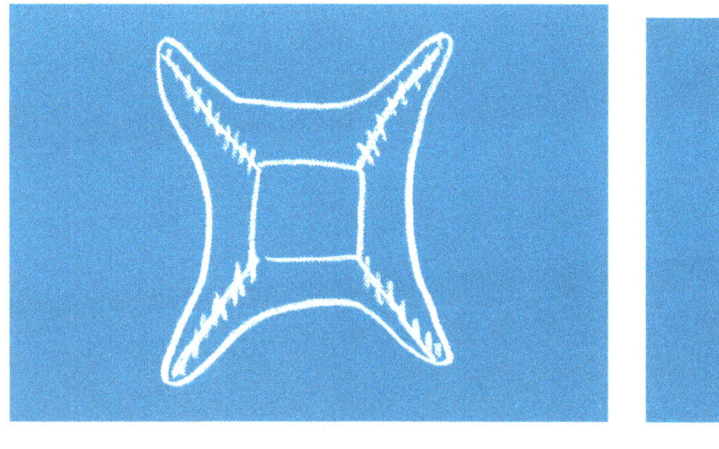

fig. 2

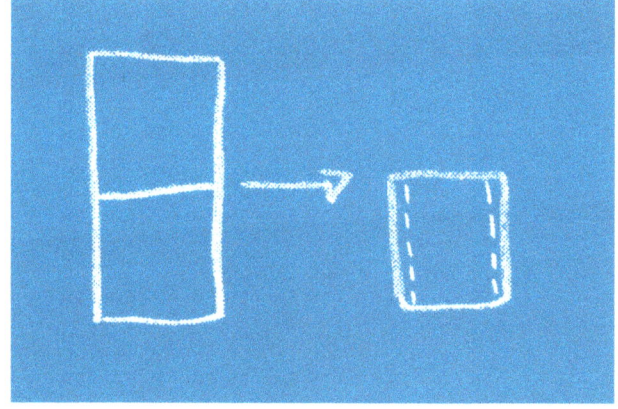

fig. 3

Step 6

Stitch along the neck and pull to gather the neck into a tight circle. Attach the head to the body and sew firmly (fig. 4).

Step 7

Sew across the ears and pull the yarn to create the shape of the ears (fig. 5).

Toy Making

fig. 4

fig. 5

Step 8

An I-cord tail is created using 2 double-pointed needles. Cast on 5 stitches and knit one row. Instead of turning your work around, slide your stitches over to the other end of the needle and knit again, keeping the working yarn across the back of your stitches. Slide and repeat until you have reached your desired length. Cast off (fig. 6). Sew the tail onto the kitten and then tuck in loose yarn ends with a tapestry needle.

You could also knit a tail by casting on 6 stitches and knitting a piece that is 2/3 of the body length. Then cast off. Sew together the edges of the tail and sew onto the body. If your kitten is small, then you might cast on fewer than 6 stitches. Always adjust according to the size of the kitten.

fig. 6

Squirrel

Toy Making

Materials

- Yarn
- Knitting needles
- Wool stuffing
- Cardboard
- Tapestry or darning needle

Step 1

Body—Cast on 25 stitches. Knit in stockinette stitch for 40 rows, cast off (fig. 1).

Step 2

Head—Cast on 18 stitches. Knit in stockinette stitch for 9 rows, cast off (fig. 1).

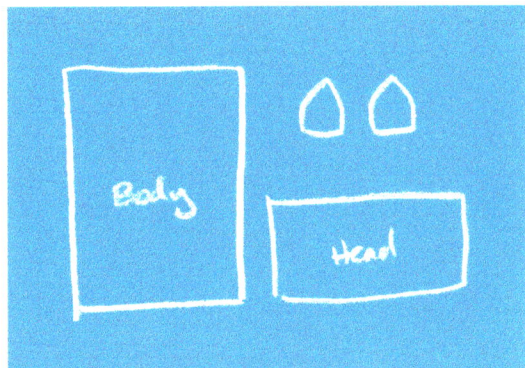

fig. 1

Step 3

Ears—Cast on 5 stitches. Knit in stockinette stitch for 2 rows, then decrease 1 stitch at the beginning of each row for 2 more rows, cast off (fig. 1).

Step 4

Body—fold the corners toward each other to create a "cone" for each leg. Leave an opening at the belly for stuffing. Stuff the body with wool. Then sew up the opening at the belly. Make sure to press wool into the corners of "cone" (fig. 2).

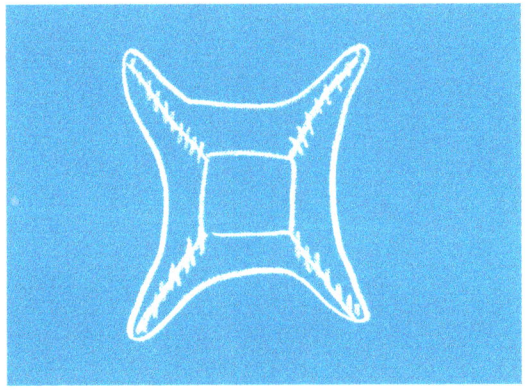

fig. 2

Squirrel

Step 5

Head—Fold the head in half to make a square. Sew two sides of the head leaving bottom side open (fig. 3). Turn right side out, rounding one corner to make the top of the head and leaving the point on one corner to create the nose (fig. 4).

Step 6

Stitch through along the neck and pull gently to gather, which will create a round neck. (fig. 4). Stuff with wool and attach to the body of the squirrel. Attach ears high and close together on the head (fig. 5).

fig. 3

fig. 4

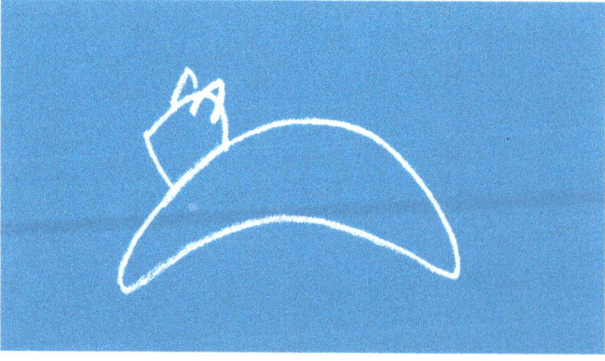

fig. 5

Step 7

To make the tail, take a rectangular piece of cardboard, sizing it in proportion to your squirrel. Wrap the yarn around the cardboard, enough to make it bushy once completed. Stitch the yarn along the middle on both sides of the cardboard, but not through the carboard (fig. 6).

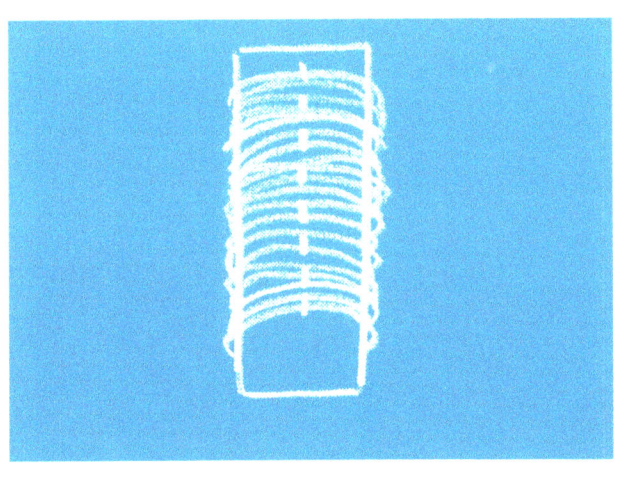

fig. 6

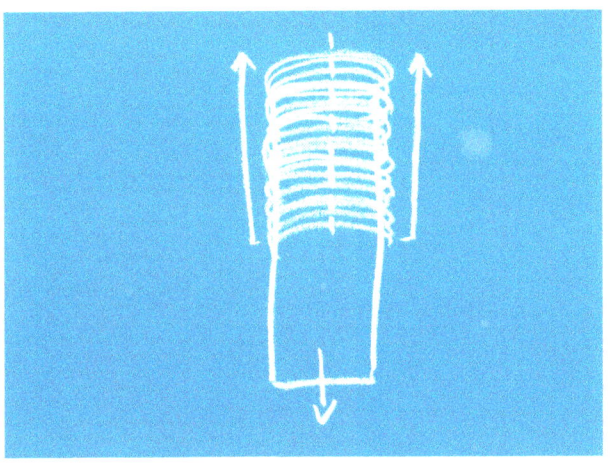

fig. 7

Step 8

Carefully slide the tail off the cardboard little by little. With each pull, sew together the front and back side of the tail together in the center to reinforce and secure the yarn (fig. 7).

Step 9

Cut the loops and trim to shape the tail. If the tail is too long, you can always fold it into itself and stitch together. Attach the tail to the body. Tuck in loose yarn ends with a tapestry or darning needle.

Leave the front paws unattached, or sew together as if the squirrel is gathering nuts.

Roly Poly

Toy Making

Simple to knit, roly polies can become so many things! They can be used to pull or wrap around objects, can be laid on the floor as roads or tracks, or can become snakes or worms…the possibilities are endless.

Materials
- Yarn
- Knitting needles

Knit in garter stitch, which allows the roly poly to lay flat and not curl at the sides. You may choose to either knit every row or purl every row. Begin with 8-10 stitches (depending on thickness of yarn) and continue until desired length. Cast off.

Play Crown

Children enjoy dressing up, and these crowns are a wonderful addition to their play wardrobe. They can also be used in other ways you would never have imagined!

Materials
- Yarn
- Knitting needles

The following instructions are given as an example, but keep in mind the size of the final crown will be different depending on the thickness of the yarn and the size of the knitting needles used. The crown will also stretch, so you will need to take that into consideration. Adjust the number of stitches, keep practicing and noting your results, and soon you will have a variety of crowns in different sizes.

Cast on 7 stitches. Knitting in garter stitch, increase 1 stitch every other row, until you have 12 stitches on the needle. Then decrease 1 stitch every other row (at the same edge as the increases) until you have 7 stitches. Repeat. Be consistent with the side on which you increase and decrease. Once the crown is the desired length, cast off and sew the cast-on and cast-off edges together. Then weave in loose yarn ends.

Heavy Hen

Children enjoy carrying heavy things. It makes them feel very proud and strong, and it is also comforting for them to feel the firmness in the soles of their feet pressed solid on the ground. A heavy hen is perfect for children to carry, care for, rest their heads on, and play with.

Use old sweaters for the Heavy Hen. It is best if they don't have a lot of stretch. You can reduce the stretch in old wool sweaters by felting them a little in the washing machine before cutting.

Materials
• 3 old wool sweaters: a large one for the hen (make sure it fits the pattern). The second sweater is for the pockets that will hold the little chicks. The third sweater is for the chicks.
• Muslin fabric with high thread count
• Wool for stuffing
• Sand
• Funnel
• Needle and thread for sewing
• Yarn and knitting needles for making the comb

Step 1

Cut two pieces from a large wool sweater using the pattern provided in the section at the back of this book. Put pieces right-side together and sew, leaving the bottom of the hen's body open. Turn right-side out. Use a running stitch to hem the bottom opening, preventing it from unraveling. This will also create the "footing" for the hen (fig. 1).

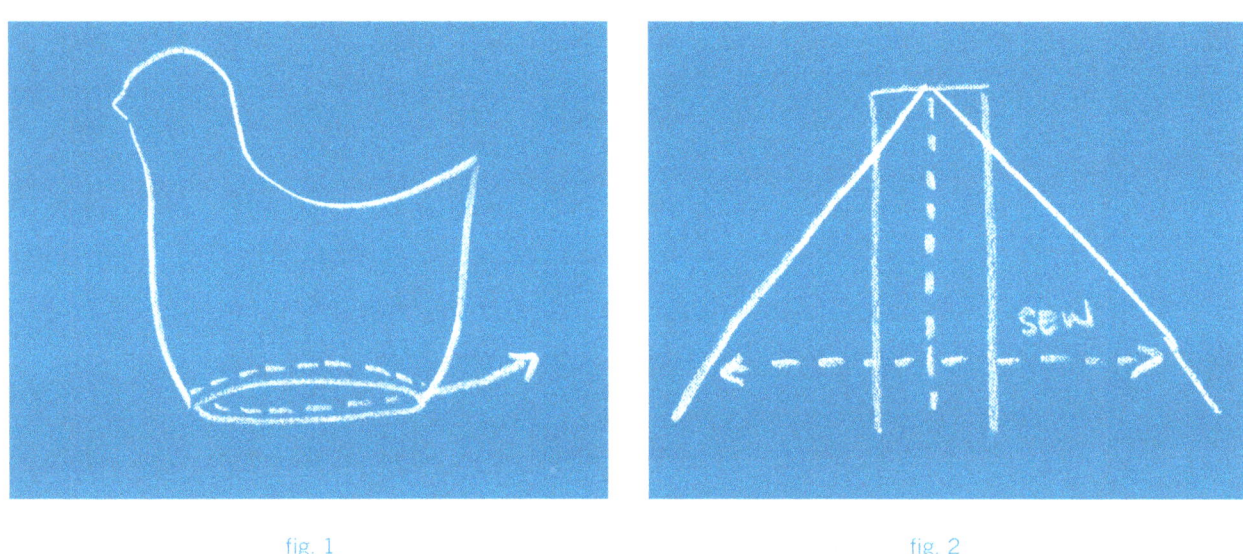

fig. 1   fig. 2

Step 2

Cut 3 pieces of muslin according to the pattern provided to create the bag that will hold the sand. Sew each bag but leave the top open so that you can create a "boxed" bottom. This will help to keep the sand bags flat.

Step 3

To create a "boxed" bottom for the bags, open one corner of the bottom to create a triangle and sew across. You will need to do this for all 3 bags (fig. 2).

Toy Making

Step 4

Turn one bag right-side out. Nest the other bags inside this bag to create a 3-layered bag. The outer bag will be the one you had turned right-side out. Fill the 3-layered bag with sand and sew up the opening at the top. Sew each layer separately. This will help prevent sand from seeping out.

Step 5

Fill the hen tightly with wool, especially around the head and neck area. You might want to use some scrap sweater fabric to fill it. This will help strengthen and firm the body and neck area. Leave a hole for the sand bag to fit firmly into place (fig. 3).

fig. 3

Step 6

Cut an oval piece of sweater fabric, ideally from the same sweater as the body, large enough to cover the opening at the bottom of the hen. Place this piece inside the opening.

Step 7

Stitch along the bottom of the hen using a running stitch (do not stitch the oval piece of sweater fabric yet, but keep it firmly in place). Once you have stitched all the way around, gently pull to gather the bottom somewhat so that it creates the base. Then sew around the opening onto the oval piece of sweater fabric to secure it and to complete the bottom.

Step 8

Pockets—Cut two pockets out of an old sweater using the pattern provided. Ideally you would cut along the bottom edge of the sweater, so that you do not have to hem the flat side of the pattern piece. This will end up being the top edge of the pocket. Pin the pockets onto the hen and hand stitch to the body using a back-stitch while folding in a quarter-inch of fabric. This hem will keep the edges of the pockets from unraveling. Leave the top open for the baby chicks to rest in (fig. 4).

fig. 4

Step 9

Baby chicks—Cut 2 pieces of sweater fabric according to the pattern provided. Put right sides of fabric together and sew around, leaving the bottom open. Turn right-side out and fill with wool. Sew the bottom closed. Sew the eyes using a dark-color thread. Repeat to make another chick.

Optional: Use red or orange yarn to knit a comb for the hen. The method is similar to making a 3-pointed crown; start with 2 stitches, then increase and decrease as you go along, fitting the comb to the size of your hen. This does not need to be precise. Then sew the comb on top of the hen's head.

Heavy Bags

Weighted bags can be square, rectangular, or even circular. These bags are a great help in developing a child's senses and imagination. Children may develop their strength and balance by carrying them, or feel the comfort of the weight pressed against their bodies. Make identical bags with different fillers to allow a child to feel the difference in weight. Nursery-age children enjoy carrying heavy items just as much as kindergarten children. The bags can be heavier for the older children and lighter for the younger ones. Most wonderful is to see two or more children working together to carry these heavy bags in their play!

Materials
- Cotton, wool, or linen fabric
  (exterior fabric)
- Muslin or other cotton fabric
  (interior fabric)
- Sand, rice, or dried beans
- Funnel
- Needle and thread for sewing

Step 1

For square bags, fold a small piece of muslin or cotton fabric in half. Cut 2 pieces of muslin or cotton fabric along the fold, so that each piece will create a square when folded (fig. 1). This will form the inside of the bag..

fig. 1

Step 2

Cut 1 square piece of cotton, wool, or linen exterior fabric along the fold in the same way as the interior fabric. This too will be a square once folded.

Step 3

Sew the two interior squares separately, but leave 2 inches open on one side. Make sure you have two identical square pieces with the open side matching (fig. 2).

fig. 2

Step 4

Turn one interior bag right-side out and place the other bag inside it to create a 2-layered bag.

Step 5

Sew exterior bag with right sides facing, leaving a two-inch opening to match the interior bag. Turn right-side out, making sure the placement of the opening matches with each layer of fabric. Place interior bag inside the exterior bag.

Step 6

Use a funnel to fill the bag with weighted material. Sew the open seams of each layer separately.

Tip: If you are using sand, make sure you use a high quality, high-thread-count cotton fabric and make a 3-layed interior bag. This will help keep the sand from seeping out.

Wool Balls

Wool balls are soft, yet they bounce! They are fun to play with and can even be made in various designs using different colors.

Materials
- Colored wool roving
- Soapy hot water
  (hot enough to touch comfortably)

Step 1

Begin with a small ball of wool, then wrap long pieces of wool tightly around it. Keep adding layers until the fluffy ball is the size of your fist. Remember, when wet-felted it will shrink in size, but you can continue to build onto the ball to make it larger.

Step 2

Saturate the fluffy ball in hot soapy water and gently roll between both hands. Continue to do this for about 10 minutes. Make sure to dip the ball in the hot soapy water again whenever the ball starts to feel cool.

Step 3

Toss the ball from one hand to the other hand, and continue to roll between both hands to help agitate the wool. This will help the wool fibers to "stick" to themselves. The ball will decrease in size but soon will firm up and begin to harden.

Tip: Begin the rolling process with light pressure. When you begin the wet-felting process with strong pressure, this will cause wool fibers to rub off and instead of sticking to the main ball, they will form chunks of fibers that hang off the ball. Once the ball begins to firm up, then you can use more pressure from your hands. But do not worry if you have "blobs" of wool fibers hanging off. You can either add another layer of wool on top to hold them in place, or cut them off.

Step 4

Once you are happy with the size of the ball, rinse with cool water and place it on a towel to dry.

Optional: Creating a Shooting Star: Cut some long strips of silk fabric on the bias. This means at an angle or diagonal to the direction of the threads (fig. 1). This prevents the fabric from fraying excessively. Once your wool ball is dry, take a couple of these strips and sew them onto the ball.

fig. 1

Resources

Joy A. Chambers, *Joy's Waldorf Dolls*, 2012

Christopher Clouder and Janni Nicol, *Creative Play for your toddler*, Gaia 2008

Bonnie Gosse and Jill Allerton, *A First Book of Knitting for Children*, Wynstones Press 2001

Bonnie Gosse and Jill Allerton, *Knitting for Children, A Second Book*, Wynstones Press 2002

Anne-Dorthe Grigaff, *Knitted Animals*, Hawthorn Press 2006

Freya Jaffke, *Toymaking with Children*, Floris Books 2010

Bernard Lievegoed, *Phases of Childhood*, Floris Books 2005

Maricristin Sealey, *Making Waldorf Dolls*, Hawthorn Press 2005

Patterns

The following patterns may be enlarged with a photocopier or hand-sketched to the dimensions indicated. Your version need not be exactly the same as the pattern; individual variations are part of the charm of these simple toys.

If you would like a PDF copy of the pattern section, you may dowload one from http://www.waldorfearlychildhood.org/toy-making-patterns.pdf.
The PDF is for your personal use only.

Projects with patterns:
- Cuddly Doll
- Formed Doll
- Small Heavy Baby
- Small Heavy Bunting
- Large Heavy Baby
- Large Heavy Bunting
- Heavy Hen

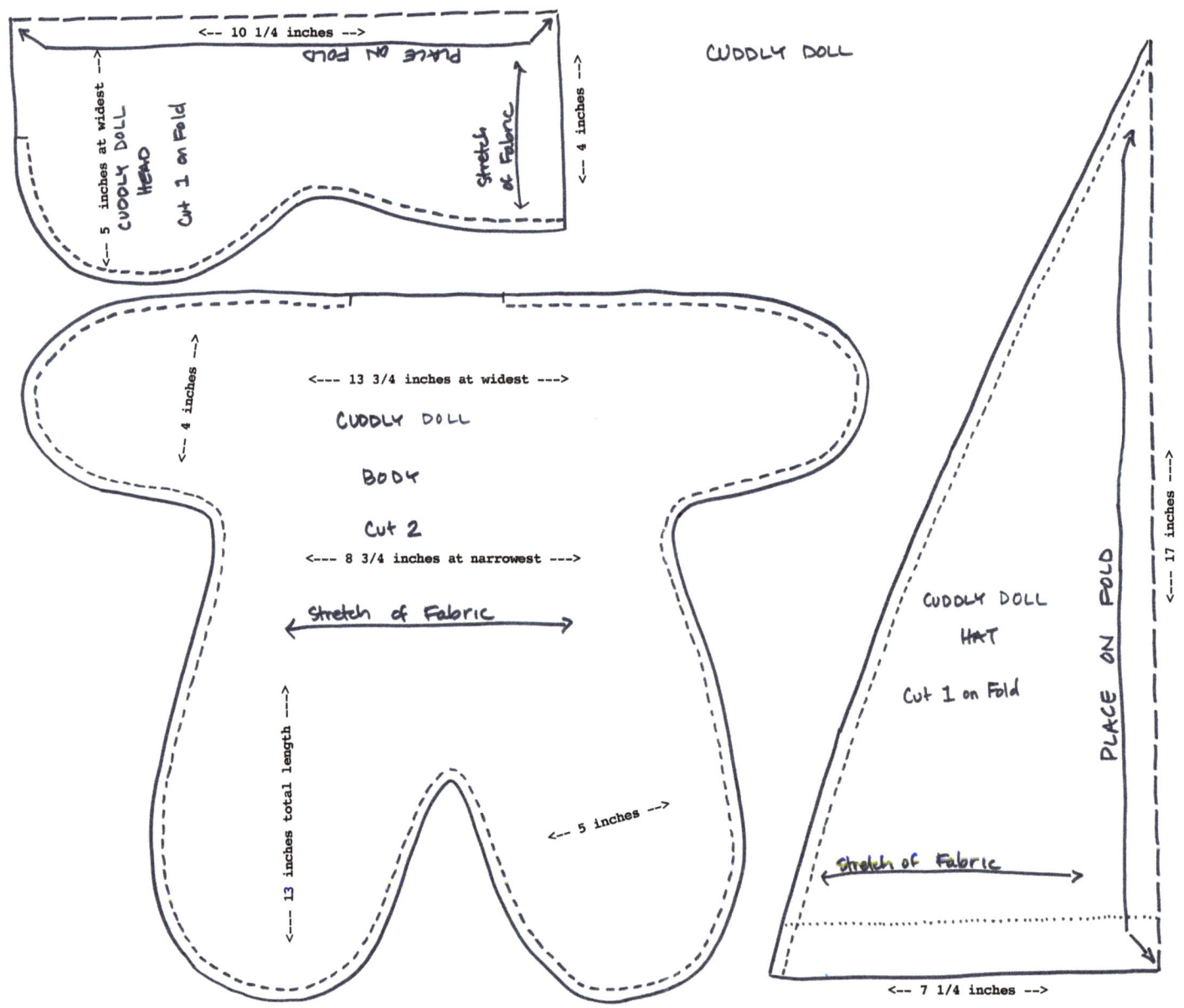

Toy Making

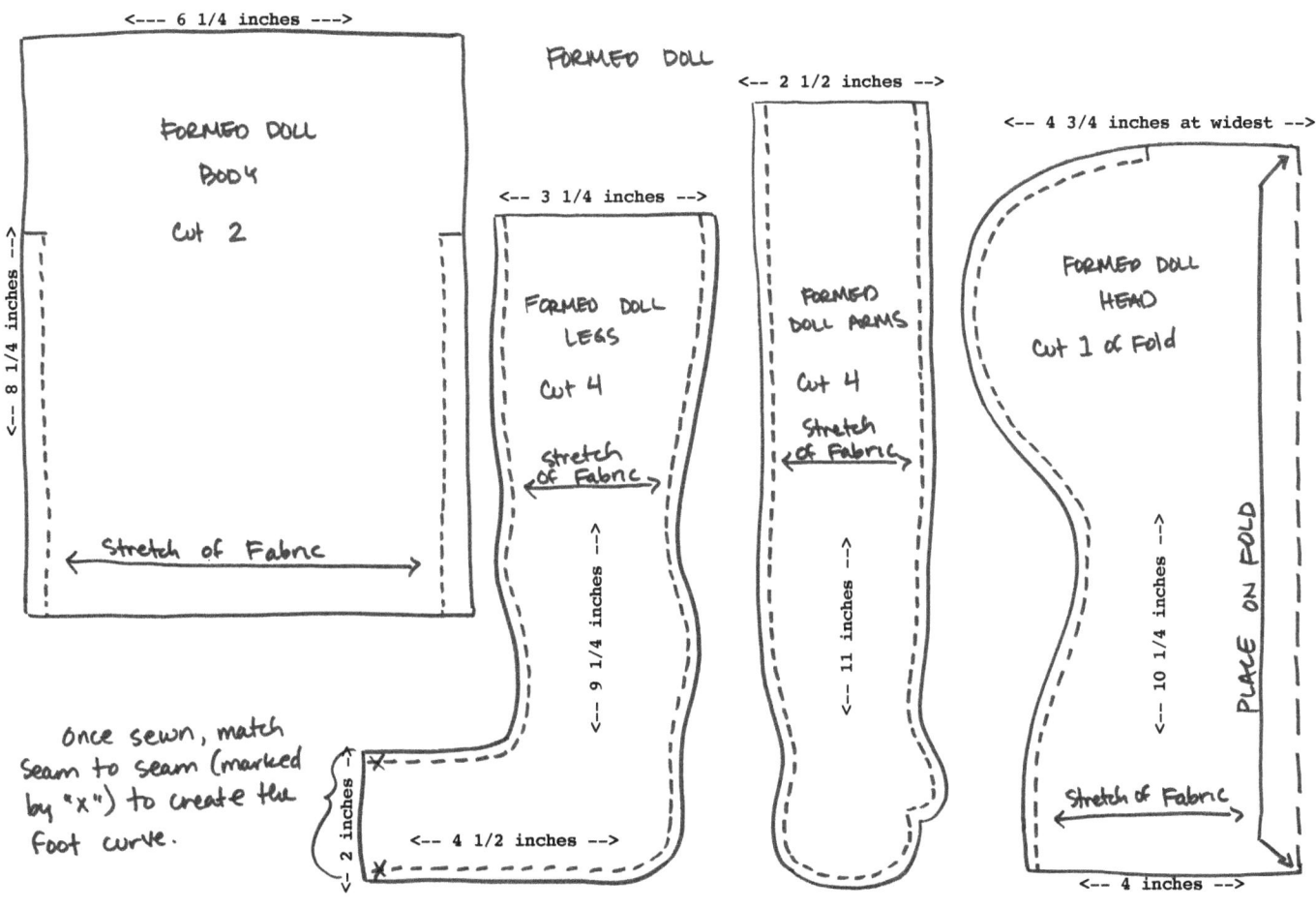

Patterns 79

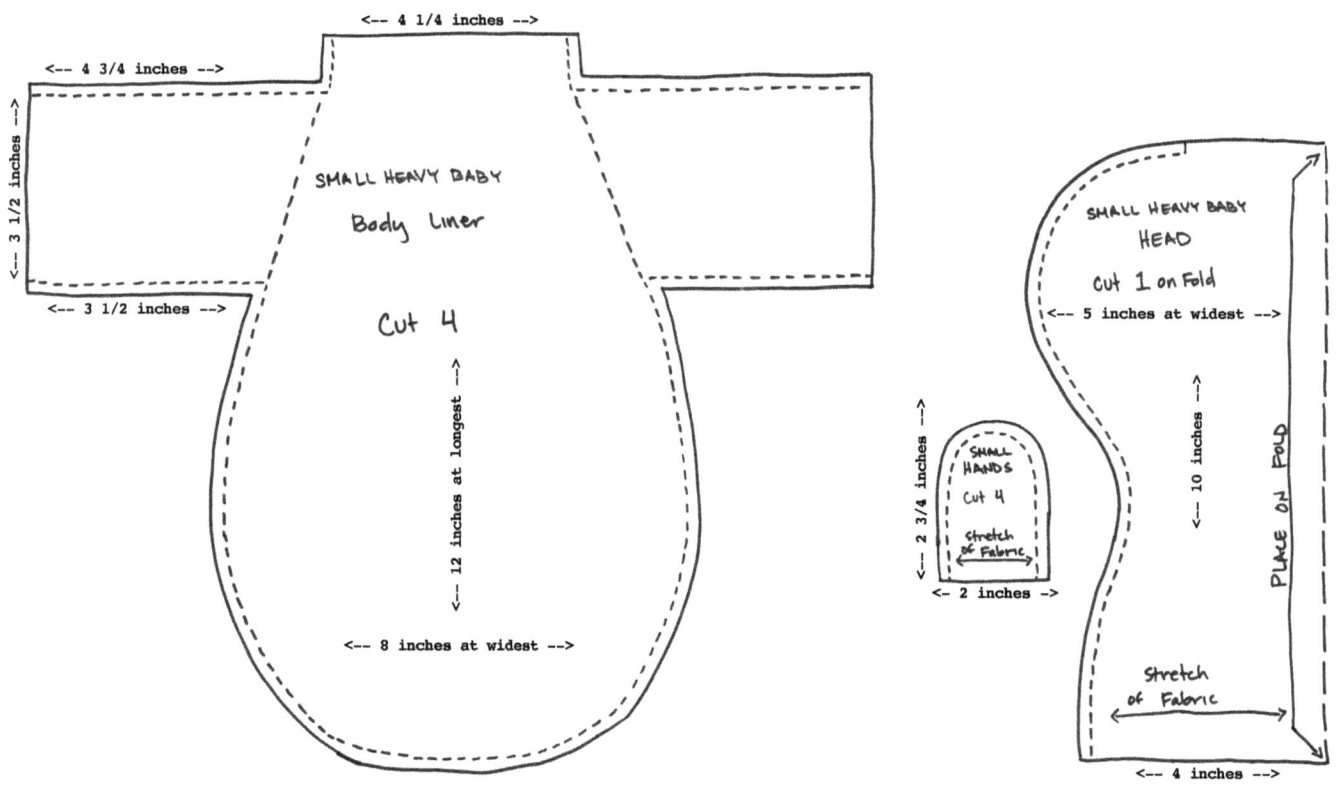

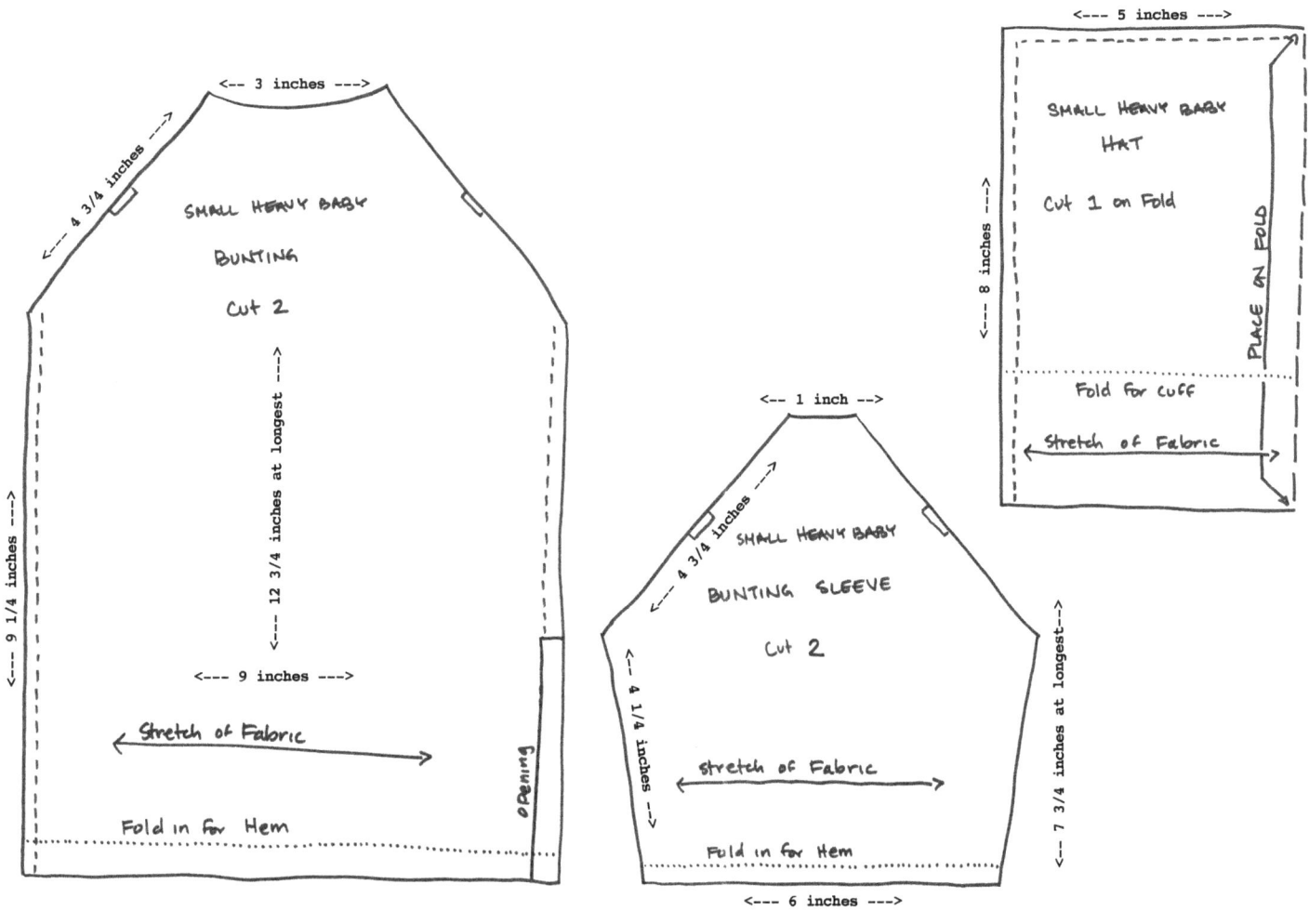

Patterns

LARGE HEAVY BABY

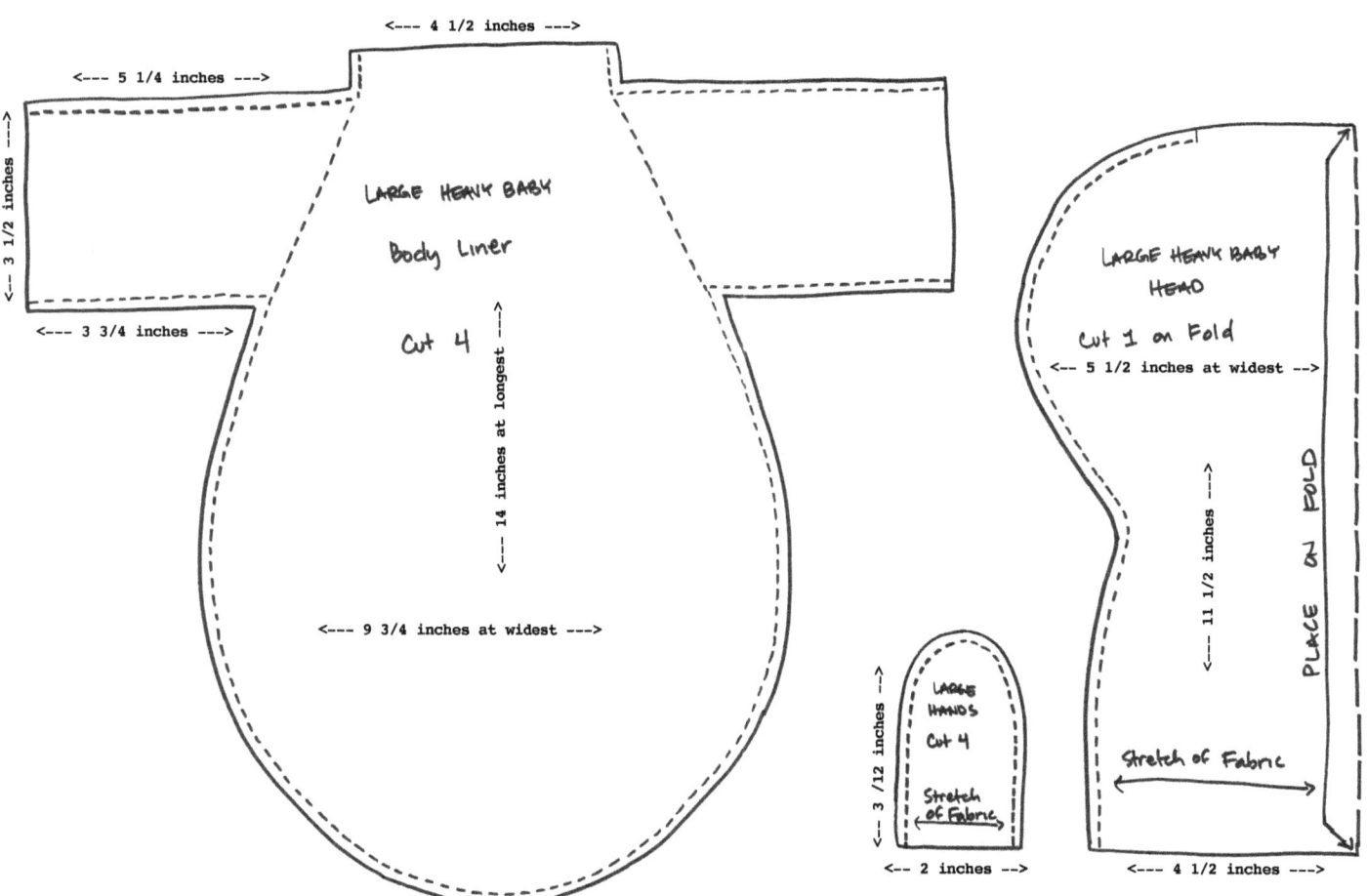

Toy Making

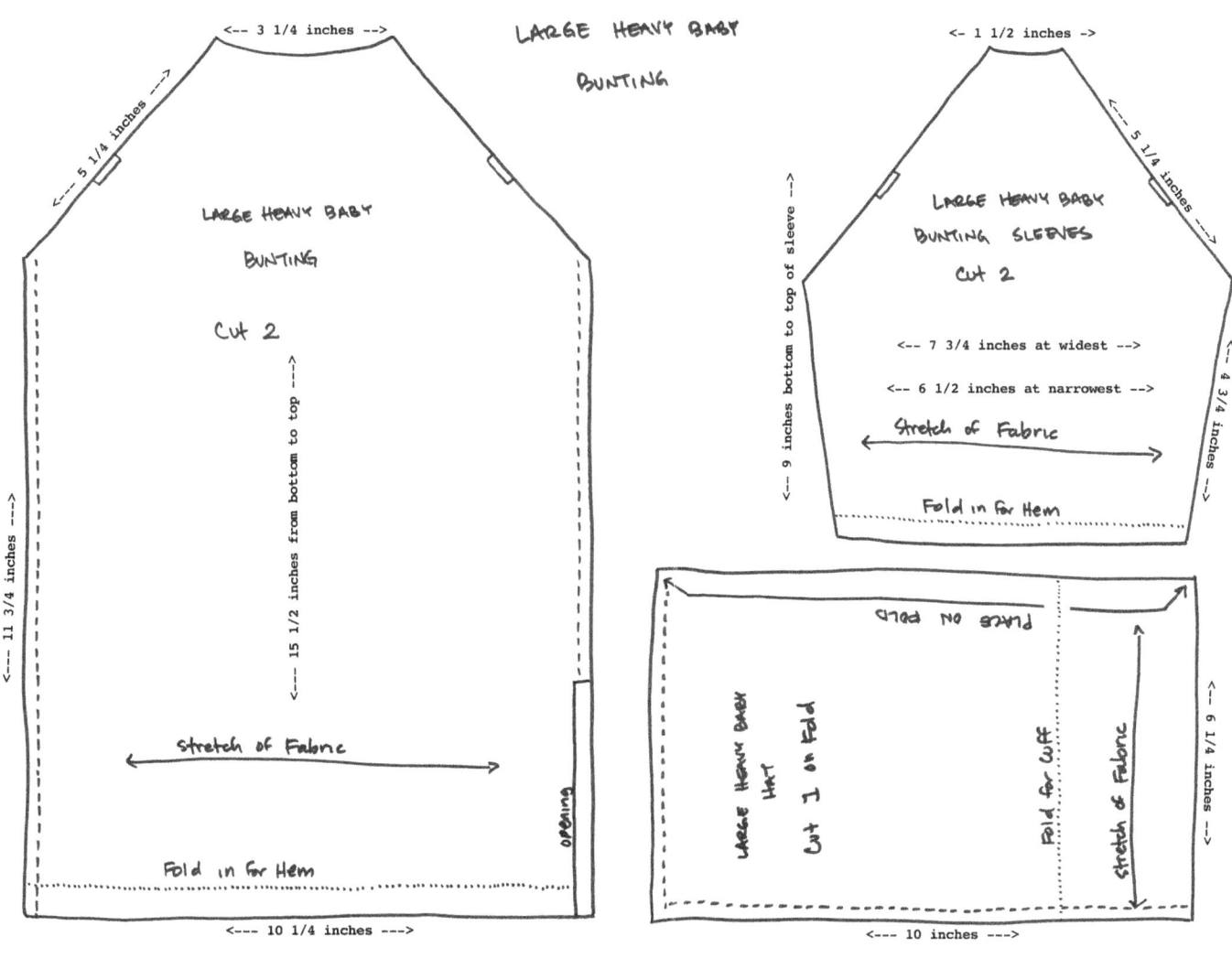

Patterns

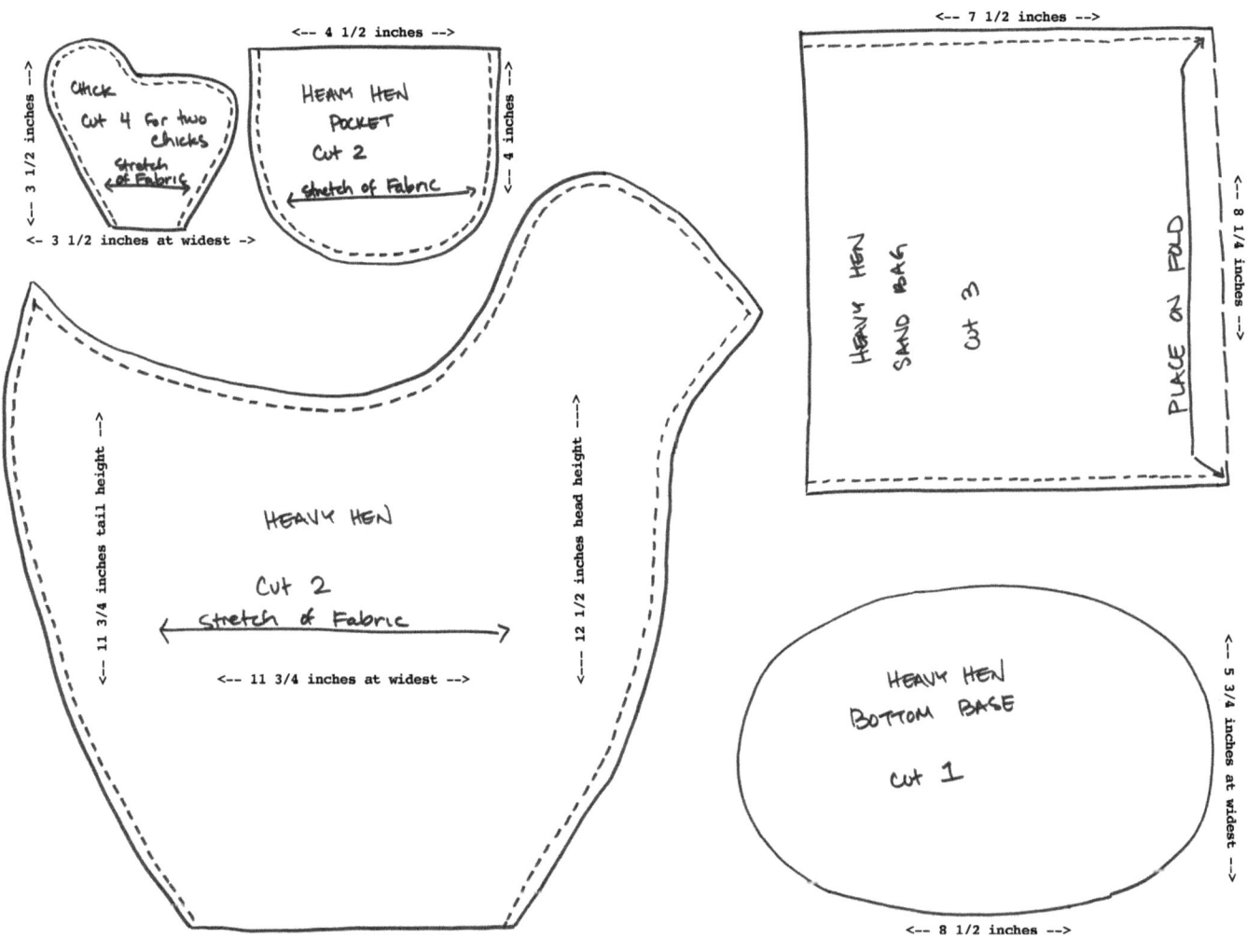